NICCOLÒ MACHIAVELLI'S

THE PRINCE

ON

THE ART OF POWER

NICCOLÒ MACHIAVELLI'S
THE PRINCE
ON
THE ART OF POWER

THE NEW ILLUSTRATED EDITION
OF THE RENAISSANCE MASTERPIECE ON LEADERSHIP

WITH AN INTRODUCTION BY CARY J. NEDERMAN

SHELTER HARBOR PRESS
NEW YORK

Niccolò Machiavelli's *The Prince* on The Art of Power

This 2017 edition first published in the USA
by Shelter Harbor Press by arrangement with EMEX Ltd

Shelter Harbor Press
603 West 115th Street, Suite 163
New York, NY 10025

For sales, contact:
info@shelterharborpress.com

Designer: Justin Ford
Picture Researcher: Julia Brown
Managing Editor: Christopher Westhorp
Managing Designer: Daniel Sturges

A CIP record for this book is available from the British Library

ISBN: 978-1-62795-099-2

10 9 8 7 6 5 4 3 2 1

Typeset in Garamond
Colour reproduction by Colourscan, Singapore
Printed in China

About the consultant
Cary J. Nederman is Professor of Political Science at Texas A & M University. Concentrating
on the history of Western political thought, with a focus on Greek, Roman, and early
European ideas up to the seventeenth century, his work illuminates the relationship
between historical traditions and contemporary concerns. He is the author or editor
of more than a dozen books and has also published over 100 articles.

Cover and page 2 captions
Cover artwork: Symbol of the city of Florence.
Page 2: Portrait of Machiavelli by Santi di Tito (1536–1603), detail. (Palazzo Vecchio, Florence/
Bridgeman Art Library.)

CONTENTS

INTRODUCTION

Niccolò Machiavelli remains one of the very few political thinkers of the past who continues to enjoy instant recognition and wide readership in the present. Despite the five centuries that separate him from us, Machiavelli's name resonates in today's popular culture as much as in the halls of academe. "Machiavellianism" (or the variant, "Machiavellism") commonly denotes a set of dispositions associated with strategic thinking, self-interest, deception, manipulation, and instrumental decision-making.[1] While moralists and preachers have long chafed against Machiavelli's conception of human conduct, psychologists and academic marketing scholars now derive important lessons about the foundations of human motivation and behaviour from his writings.[2] Machiavelli has lately been invoked as inspiration for mass-market books on subjects as varied as fashion, management, the ministry, gambling, gender roles, and international conflict.[3] Machiavelli's wisdom was not long ago contraposed to the teachings of Jesus; his insights purport to guide the moguls and hits-makers of Hollywood and the music business.[4] A computer game that applies Machiavellian precepts to the tactical conflicts of Renaissance Italy appeared during the mid-1990s.[5]

Machiavelli's enduring reputation today is built almost entirely upon his composition of a single, short, and rapidly written book, *The Prince* — a treatise that was not even published until five years after his death. It should be noted that the meaning and application of the term "prince" was very different in Machiavelli's day than in our own. The English word "prince" derives from Latin *princeps*, which was employed generically during the Middle Ages and Renaissance to describe the rule of a single person (usually a man, although it could be extended even to queens and other female rulers). It might be applied to an array of lords, stretching from local seigneurs all the way to the "universal" Holy Roman Emperor. In contrast to terms such as "king" (*rex*), "monarch" (*monarchus*), and "emperor" (*imperator*), all of which conveyed more specific types of one-person rule, *princeps* was usually deployed in order to capture the common elements shared by all such regimes. Furthermore, the word "prince" could be employed to denote a pope or other high ecclesiastical official as well as purely secular rulers. In sum, *princeps* had a highly elastic connotation. Machiavelli's choice of this title for his book reflects the general usage of his times, although he narrows his topic, as we shall see, to one specific type of "prince," namely, a ruler who acquires his position by his own skills, talents, and efforts alone.

The historical Machiavelli was in fact a far more complex and intricate thinker than those familiar only with *The Prince* might realize (as Thomas Macaulay emphasizes in his magisterial essay reprinted as an appendix to the present volume). Machiavelli left behind a vast body of writings on political affairs and philosophy as well as plays, histories, poems, biographical sketches, speeches, and many short works on a bewildering array of topics. Would the Machiavelli whose career of public service and literary production was so diverse and vigorous have recognized himself in the reputation he has acquired on account of *The Prince*? Or, to put it another way, was Machiavelli himself a Machiavellian? In all likelihood, as we shall see, Machiavelli would have understood himself quite differently from the reputation he has since acquired.

Machiavelli before *The Prince*

Relatively little is known for certain about Machiavelli's early life in comparison with many important figures of the Italian Renaissance.[6] He was born on 3 May 1469 in Florence and at a young age became a pupil of a renowned Latin teacher, Paolo da Ronciglione. It is speculated that he attended the University of Florence, and even a cursory glance at his corpus reveals that he received at least the rudiments of a Renaissance humanistic education. Machiavelli's writings do not assist us very much, however, in recovering the specifics of the curriculum he followed. That he knew of most of the important classical Latin authors – rhetoricians, historians, orators, and philosophers – is clear enough from direct or oblique references to them in his writings. It also seems that he was familiar with the main philosophers and historians of Greek antiquity (albeit probably in translation), as well as with the major pre-humanist (such as Dante and Petrarch) and humanist authors writing in Italian and Latin between 1300 and 1500.[7]

Yet if Machiavelli was a man of some erudition, he thrived first and foremost in the world of public affairs. Only once he entered into politics, with his appointment as the Second Chancellor of the Republic of Florence in 1498, do we receive a fuller and more accurate picture of his life. To appreciate the climate within which Machiavelli's political vision was shaped, we need to grasp briefly the political landscape of Italy around 1500. The peninsula was dotted with dozens of semi-autonomous city states, ruled either by dynastic clans (such as the Medici family in Florence) or by some form of self-governing quasi-popular body styled after the traditions of the ancient republics (and especially Rome). These city states entered into an intricate and ever-shifting set of political and military alliances and pacts, built around the four "great powers" of northern and central Italy: the Duchy of Milan, the Republic of Venice, the city of Florence, and the Roman Papacy. The major players on the Italian scene in turn often depended on the resources of other European states – France, Spain, and the Holy Roman Empire, most especially – in order to achieve their strategic goals.

Florence had been governed by a republican constitution since 1494, when the Medici family and its supporters were driven from power as the result of a complex set of military and political machinations occasioned by the invasion of the French king, Charles VIII. While the Florentine Republic initially was under the sway of the charismatic preacher Fra Girolamo Savonarola, his execution in 1498 paved the way for a more stable form of self-government to emerge. Machiavelli was among the leading magistrates serving post-Medici republican Florence. In his role as secretary, first to the Ten of War (the Florentine body charged with coordinating the city's relations with foreign powers), and thereafter to the Nine of the Militia, Machiavelli's duties alternated between planning the city's military strategy and engaging in diplomacy. For example, he is commonly credited with reviving the Florentine militia as an alternative to the city's long-standing reliance on allies and mercenaries for troops. As a diplomat, in particular, Machiavelli seems to have excelled. For fourteen years, he travelled widely, representing Florence and her interests to the major leaders of Italy as well as to the royal court of France and to the Holy Roman imperial curia of Maximilian. In this capacity, he observed many of the famous and infamous figures of early sixteenth-century Europe, including those (such as King Louis XII of France, Cesare Borgia, and Pope Julius II) who became central objects of study in his political works. His extant correspondence, dispatches, and essays of commentary from these early years testify to the facility with which he handled his delicate political assignments, not to mention his acute talent for understanding and analysing the personalities and institutions he came into contact with. These writings also provide important source materials that Machiavelli mined as examples for his political reflections in *The Prince*. We find in them an appraisal of the tactics used by successful governments as well as recommendations for how the political masters of Florence might best ensure the city's safety in the midst of the diplomatic and military posturing of its friends and enemies.

In 1502, the Florentine Republic's Great Council authorized the executive position of *gonfaloniere* (or chief administrator for life), to which Machiavelli's political patron and mentor, Piero Soderini, was appointed. During the following decade, Machiavelli thrived and his influence and prestige grew. The situation was not to last, however. In 1512, with the assistance of Spanish troops, the Medici defeated the Republic's armed forces and dissolved the government. Machiavelli was a direct victim of the regime change. In early November 1512, he was removed from his position in the chancery and placed in a form of internal exile; worse still, in February 1513 he was imprisoned and tortured for several weeks as a result of (incorrect) suspicions about his involvement in a conspiracy against the Medici. His retirement thereafter to his farm outside Florence afforded the occasion and the impetus for him to turn to literary pursuits.

Author of *The Prince*

The first of Machiavelli's major writings from his period of political exile is also ultimately the one most often associated with his name: *The Prince*. Written during the latter part of 1513 (and perhaps early 1514), but only published posthumously in 1532, *The Prince* was composed in great haste by an author who was, among other things, seeking to regain his status in the Florentine government. (Many who had held office under the Republic were quickly rehabilitated and returned to service under the Medici.) In a letter to his friend and former colleague Francesco Vettori, dated 10 December 1513,[8] Machiavelli describes his composition of a "little book *De principatibus*" (referring to the original Latin title of *The Prince*), which sets out to "discuss what a principality is, how many different types there are, how they are gained, how they are held, why they are lost." Machiavelli denies that its main teachings are directly his own, but instead reflect his gleanings from a nightly imagined "conversation" among members of "the ancient courts of the men of old," who invite him to listen to their discourses and who even permit their guest "to ask them why they acted as they did, and out of kindness they respond."

In the same letter, Machiavelli debates the pros and cons of presenting the results to the new head of the Florentine wing of the Medici, Giuliano de'Medici. He feared that the book might not be read by its intended audience and would instead fall into the hands of his enemies, who might use it against him. In the event, whether before or after Giuliano's death in early 1516, Machiavelli apparently decided to pursue formal presentation and wrote the letter of dedication (see pages 24–25) that we now possess to the subsequent Medici lord, Lorenzo de'Medici, who almost certainly did not read it when it finally came into his hands.[9]

It is commonplace, and not entirely inaccurate, to say that Machiavelli wrote *The Prince* as a sort of extended job application, a résumé in support of his effort to rehabilitate himself politically. From first to last, he promises to reveal "hidden knowledge" about how its princely reader might learn to govern successfully (especially as a "new" ruler) that no other counselor would teach. We know from his letters that almost immediately after he was removed in 1512, and for the rest of his life, he engaged in a non-stop campaign to return to active service in Florentine government. *The Prince* may rightly be understood as one prong in this pursuit. Yet even after he had finished writing the main part of the treatise, as he expressed in his 10 December 1513 letter to Vettori (see above), Machiavelli remained ambivalent about whether he should in fact present it to the ruling Medici house. Perhaps he was scared that his ideas were too novel, too extreme, for the audience he envisioned to appreciate.

This leaves open, then, the vexed question of what Machiavelli actually desired to achieve by composing *The Prince*. Many politicians and moralists, no less than scholars, have tried to distil the "essence" of the work. But a combination of intentions surely swirled about in Machiavelli's mind, so that the question of his goals resists any single simple answer. One obvious aim was a measure of personal self-consolation that stemmed from his attempt to boil down the lessons of his political career into a concise and clearly stated treatise. As Machiavelli says both in the letter to Vettori and in the text of *The Prince* itself, he did not wish his career's experiences to be forgotten either by him or by others. Even if he could not realise his own return to a position of power, he believed that his accrued wisdom, based on years of direct acquaintance with the actual ways in which political rule was conducted by his contemporaries, afforded useful insights that might be employed to obtain dominance. Thus, Machiavelli offers a summary of what might be learnt from careful and realistic observation of the politics of his day.

As a man who valued above all else the quest for "glory," that is, the attainment of posthumous memory in historical time as reward for the performance of great deeds, *The Prince* reflects the crystallization of his own agenda as a political creature who craved recognition for his accomplishments.

At the same time, *The Prince* may properly be read to convey more nefarious and even subversive lessons. In the eighteenth century, the French-Swiss philosopher Jean-Jacques Rousseau recognized that the treatise taught lessons for the citizens of republics about the dark side of princely government, namely, that a successful monarch must be prepared to engage in all manner of immorality and deceit, even as he appeared to uphold conventional pieties.[10] Machiavelli possessed a notoriously playful (and even pointed) sense of humour; there are many remarks in *The Prince* that ring more truly of satire than of serious counsel. For example, sections such as Chapter XVIII ("Concerning the Way in Which Princes Should Keep Faith") contain wicked parody of the traditional literature of "advice to princes," a genre pioneered during the Latin Middle Ages and continued by many Renaissance authors, that promised to teach rulers the path to both political success and eternal salvation by learning conformity with moral and religious rectitude.[11] By contrast, Machiavelli preferred *virtù* (a word properly translated into English by such terms as "talent," "skill," "ability," and "prowess," but seldom "virtue" in an ethical sense), a personal quality demanding a flexibility of moral character that is seldom (if ever) within the scope of human psychology.[12] The ruler of *virtù* could not afford the luxury of moral certainty or probity.

According to a still more extreme interpretation, *The Prince* may be viewed as a work designed precisely to undermine the dominance of the Medici.[13] It has been pointed out that, should Machiavelli's advice be taken at face value, the treatise recommends that the Medici engage in conduct that is self-defeating and ruinous, such as his suggestions that the prince should live openly among his populace and that ordinary citizens should be armed. This reading is sustained by critical examination of the relationship between the advice Machiavelli offers and the consequences of following that counsel. If we accept that Machiavelli was a republican who was interested in the destruction of the Medici or, at any rate, in their political marginalization, *The Prince* may be understood not merely as an expression of a political agenda, but as a political act itself. The tract's meaning is therefore entirely an act of deception, aimed to restore the republic even as it counsels the prince. In particular, the ruler is given self-contradictory advice that, if followed, would lead him to engage in self-destructive conduct. There are numerous personal factors that would have led Machiavelli to write such a ruse. He knew first-hand how dangerous the appearance of disloyalty to the Medici could be; he thus crafted his counsel slyly, yet with the ultimate goal of dislodging the enemy and restoring republican rule.

None of these readings of *The Prince* is likely to attain final confirmation. The work, like its author, is too nuanced and multi-faceted to admit a single definitive interpretation. And, indeed, precisely this capaciousness of interpretation (along with the provocative quality of Machiavelli's rhetoric) is why *The Prince* continues to enjoy such a wide audience in the modern day.

Later writings

Machiavelli moved on from *The Prince*. His enforced retire-ment led him to other literary endeavours. He wrote verse and short prose; his stage comedies, *La Mandragola* and *Clizia*, proved popular as satires of seduction and deception, illustrating perhaps more graphically than *The Prince* the foibles of human nature. (These are discussed at some length in Macaulay's classic essay in the appendix.) He also penned a study of *The Art of War* (published in 1521), which systematizes the fundamentals of combat that he learned during his service to the Florentine republic. Notably, his analysis applies the idea of *virtù* to the situation of the field commander. A successful general, like a successful prince, must know how to adjust his strategies to the on-the-ground conditions that he encounters. Disaster awaits any commander who insists upon following a pre-set battle plan without regard to the terrain, to the material and human circumstances of his own forces, and to the strengths and weaknesses of the enemy.

Most importantly, during his waning years, Machiavelli composed his other major contribution to political thought, the *Discourses on the Ten Books of Titus Livy*, an exposition of the principles of republican rule masquerading as a commentary on the work of the famous historian of the Roman Republic. Unlike *The Prince*, the three books of the *Discourses* were authored over a long period of time (commencing in 1514 or 1515 and completed in 1518 or 1519, although only published posthumously in 1531). The ideas contained in the book may have been shaped by informal discussions attended by Machiavelli among some of the leading Florentine intellectual and political figures under the sponsorship of Cosimo Rucellai, to whom he dedicated the *Discourses*. During the later sixteenth and seventeenth centuries, the *Discourses* enjoyed a readership on a par with *The Prince*. Indeed, it seems reasonable to imagine that, had Machiavelli never written *The Prince* or had he suppressed it, his reputation as a leading political thinker would have been secured by the encomium to and defense of republican government contained in the *Discourses*.

Machiavelli persisted in his desire to return to some role in public service. Probably as a result of the aid of well-connected friends whom he never stopped appealing to for intervention, Machiavelli began to gain favor with the Medici. In 1520, he was commissioned by Cardinal Giulio de' Medici to compose a *History of Florence*, an assignment completed in 1525 and presented to the cardinal, who had since become Pope Clement VII. Machiavelli's ability to complete this task without affronting the Medici clan was likely a litmus test of his reliability. Although the *History of Florence* has been mined for evidence of some subversive or disloyal tendencies, it seems to reflect the "trustworthy and disinterested" character that Machiavelli ascribed to himself in the 10 December 1513 letter to Vettori. As a result, other small duties were forthcoming from the Medici family, but before he could be fully restored to their good graces, he died on 21 June 1527. He is buried in Santa Croce in Florence.

The return to republican populism

Any fair and balanced appreciation of the historical and intellectual merits of *The Prince* requires some attention to the republican ideals espoused in the *Discourses on the Ten Books of Titus Livy*. While *The Prince* is doubtless the most widely read of Machiavelli's works, the *Discourses* perhaps most honestly express his personal political beliefs and commitments, in particular his republican sympathies. The *Discourses* certainly draws upon the same reservoir of language and concepts that fed *The Prince*, but the former treatise leads to conclusions quite different from – many readers have said contradictory to – the latter. In particular, *The Prince* implies that the best princely regime is one in which both ruler and subjects live securely, with a strong government which holds in check the aspirations of all segments of the populace by means of legal and institutional mechanisms. In the republican regime preferred in the *Discourses*, however, the goal of the political order is the freedom of the community, created by the active participation of and contention between the major forces within it, namely the nobility and the people. The liberty of the whole republic, for Machiavelli, depends upon the liberty of its component parts. While customarily the blame for the collapse of the Roman Republic had been assigned to warring factions that eventually destroyed it, Machiavelli holds that precisely the same conflicts generated a "creative tension" that was the source of Roman liberty. The "tumults" between the elites and the populace directly generated the good laws of Rome and the virtuous conduct of its citizens.[14] Machiavelli thought that other republican models (such as those adopted by Sparta or Venice), which valued the power of the nobility to the exclusion of the popular faction, necessarily produce weaker and less successful political systems, ones that are either stagnant or prone to decay when circumstances change.

Machiavelli evinces particular confidence in the capacity of the people to contribute to the promotion of communal liberty. In the *Discourses*, he ascribed to the masses a quite extensive competence to judge and act for the public good in various settings, explicitly contrasting the "prudence and stability" of ordinary citizens with the unsound discretion of the prince.[15] This is not an arbitrary expression of personal preference on Machiavelli's part. He maintains that the people are more concerned about, and more willing to defend, liberty than either princes or nobles.[16] Whereas the latter tend to conflate their liberty with their ability to dominate and control others, the masses are more concerned with protecting themselves against oppression and consider themselves "free" when they are not abused, or threatened with such abuse, by the more powerful.[17] In turn, when they fear the onset of such oppression, ordinary citizens are more inclined to object and to defend the common liberty. Such an active role for the people, while necessary for the maintenance of vital public liberty, is fundamentally antithetical to the hierarchical structure of subordination-and-rule on which princely governments rest. The preconditions of a free common life simply do not favor the security that is the aim of monarchy.

Machiavelli's praise for the role of the people in securing the republic is supported by his confidence in the generally illuminating effects of public speech upon the citizenry. Near the beginning of the first *Discourse*, he notes that some may object to the extensive freedom enjoyed by the Roman people to assemble, to protest, and to veto laws and policies. But he responds that the liberty of the Romans depended crucially upon popular mechanisms of deliberation and decision-making. Machiavelli thus praised a key feature of classical republicanism: the competence of the people to respond to and to support the words of the gifted orator when he speaks truly about the public welfare. Elsewhere in the *Discourses*, he argued for the superiority of popular over princely government on the grounds that the people are well ordered and hence "prudent, stable and grateful," so long as room is made for public speech and deliberation within the community. Citing the widely known Roman maxim *vox populi, vox dei* ("the voice of the people is the voice of God"), Machiavelli insisted that the people are not only competent to discern the best course of action when orators lay out competing plans, but they are in fact better qualified to make decisions than are princes.[18] Likewise, should the people depart from the law-abiding path, they may readily be convinced to restore order. The contrast Machiavelli draws is striking. The republic governed by words and persuasion – in sum, ruled by public speech – is almost sure to realize the common good of its citizens; and, even should it err, recourse is always available to further discourse. Princely regimes, because they exclude or limit open discussion, ultimately rest upon coercive domination and can only be corrected by violent means.

Machiavelli's legacy

So, to return to the question with which this introduction began, was Machiavelli a Machiavellian? It should be obvious that there are many twists and turns involved in giving any feasible answer. If Machiavellianism connotes crass opportunism in the name of acquiring or maintaining power for its own sake, then Machiavelli does not deserve to be tarred with the brush of his own name. He evinced throughout his life an unwavering commitment to certain firm beliefs about ultimate political values, which he in turn was able to articulate and to defend cogently. Machiavelli was without doubt a convinced republican who held that there were good reasons – practical as well as moral – for the institution of self-government in preference to princely regimes.

On the other hand, Machiavelli acknowledged that there are degrees in the judgment of political affairs. He declined, unlike Plato or other ancient or modern philosophers, to insist that a single type of government or constitutional order afforded the only viable way of living. Rather, Machiavelli made more fine-grained distinctions, so that he was prepared to countenance forms of political conduct that others rejected out of hand. He doubted human capacities for achieving ideal results, but he did not descend into the basest sort of cynicism. He balanced his negative evaluation of what human beings could achieve as individuals with a chastened optimism about what they might be able to accomplish collectively. Hence, Machiavelli could without contradiction accept the necessities that accompanied inferior forms of government such as principalities without dismissing the aspirations of republican regimes to provide liberty for their citizens.

The ambivalent aspects of Machiavelli's thought and writings in turn resulted in a wide variety of fates for his reputation. His work was widely republished, disseminated and read in the years following his death, even after the inclusion of his entire corpus on the Index of Prohibited Books by the papacy in 1559.[19] On the one hand, his supposed immoralism was reviled by a vast array of critics, including not least the Prussian crown prince Frederick, who composed a treatise called the *Anti-Machiavel* in the middle of the eighteenth century. In this vein, Machiavelli was both lauded and condemned for his supposed formulation of the doctrine of *raison d'etat* (reason of state), which placed so-called "political realism" at the forefront of justifications for the state to act instrumentally for its own good, without regard for constraints of religious piety and moral convention.[20] Even today, one of the most common schools of interpretation concerning Machiavelli depicts him as a "teacher of evil" and proponent of tyranny who not merely rejected the role of ethical considerations in politics, but even revelled in the use of cruelty, treachery, and violence as worthy political techniques.[21]

On the other hand, the republican dimension of Machiavelli's thought enjoyed an equally strong reception. The diffusion of Machiavelli's republican thought has been observed throughout the so-called Atlantic world and, specifically, in the ideas that guided the framers of the American constitution regarding the inevitability of factions and the construction of a system of checks and balances.[22] The *Discourses* were reprinted at least as often as *The Prince* from the sixteenth century onwards and received wide praise as an antidote to the view of Machiavelli as a "murderous" author. At the same time, there has been deep dispute about the specific nature of the republican theory that Machiavelli propounded. According to some authors, his republicanism is of a civic humanist variety whose roots are to be found in classical antiquity; Machiavelli is therefore the primary source for conveying a political tradition with a considerable pedigree.[23] Others have stressed the profound modernity of the intellectual substance of Machiavellian republicanism.[24]

Such disagreement about the character of Machiavelli's republicanism raises the broader problem of his relationship to his intellectual sources and historical context and thus of his "originality" (a topic examined at length in the essay by Sir Isaiah Berlin in the appendix). Cases have been made for and against Machiavelli's political morality, his conception of the state, his religious views, and many other features of his work as forming the distinctive basis for the "originality" of his contribution. Yet few firm conclusions can be drawn. One reasonable explanation for the intractability of the "originality" issue is that Machiavelli was effectively trapped between innovation and tradition, between *via antiqua* and *via moderna*, in a way that generated conceptual tensions within his thought as a whole and even within individual texts.[25] Such historical ambiguity permits Machiavelli's readers to make equally convincing cases for contradictory claims about his fundamental stance without appearing to commit egregious violence to his doctrines.

This is not to say that Machiavelli was fundamentally inconsistent. Rather, the apparently conflicting features of his thought may be credited to his attempt to innovate by means of looking back to widely known historical examples and genres of political writing, while at the same time seeking to draw different conclusions from the commonplace expectations of his audience. Thus, he could not avoid the incorporation of important elements of precisely the conventions he was challenging. For example, in Chapter XVIII of *The Prince*, he seems to advise would-be rulers to prepare themselves for the commission of immorality in order to succeed, yet he never explicitly proposes (as many have supposed) that evil actions are worthy or meritorious in themselves. This may seem a contradiction, but it is perhaps best understood as a reflection of the fact that Machiavelli cannot bring himself to reverse totally the standard moral convictions of his day. In spite of his repeated assertion

of his own originality, his careful attention to pre-existing traditions meant that he was never fully able to escape his intellectual confines. Thus, Machiavelli might best be understood as si-
multaneously "original" and "conventional," as both an "ancient"
and a "modern," a thinker of great vision who still remained
deeply indebted to the context within which he wrote.

CARY J. NEDERMAN

NOTES FOR INTRODUCTION

[1] For a useful survey, see Ben-Ami Scharfstein, *Amoral Politics: The Persistent Truth of Machiavellianism* (Albany: State University of New York Press, 1995).

[2] See Phil Harris, Andrew Lock and Patricia Rees, *Machiavelli, Marketing, and Management* (London: Routledge, 2000); Richard W. Byrne and Andrew Whiten, *Machiavellian Intelligence: Social Expertise and the Evolution of Intellect in Monkeys, Apes, and Humans* (Oxford: Oxford University Press, 1989).

[3] Nicholas Antongiavanni, *The Suit: A Machiavellian Approach to Men's Style* (New York: Collins, 2006); Lynn F. Gunlicks, *The Machiavellian Manager's Handbook for Success* (Lincoln, NE: Writer's Club Press, 2000); Brandon L. Lovely, *A Machiavellian View of the Ministry: A Guide for Professional Leaders of Voluntary Organizations* (New York: Vantage Press, 1988); David Apostolico, *Machiavellian Poker Stretegy: How to Play Like a Prince and Rule the Poker Table* (Seacaucus, NJ: Lyle Stuart, 2005); Nick Casanova, *The Machiavellian's Guide to Womanizing* (New York: Carrol & Graf, 1995); Robert Franklin, *The Princess: How Daddy's Little Girl Can Survive and Thrive in the Machiavellian New Millennium* (Lincoln, NE: Writer's Club Press, 2000); Obadiah Shoher, *Samson Blinded: A Machiavellian Perspective on the Middle East Conflict* (Charleston, SC: BookSurge Publishing, 2006).

[4] Stanley Bing, *What Would Machiavelli Do? The Ends Justify the Meanness* (New York: Collins, 2002); Nick Paumgarten, "Fresh Prince: Hip-hop's Machiavelli" in *The New Yorker* (6 November 2006), pp. 56-66.

[5] The game, called "Machiavelli the Prince," was distributed by the now-defunct company MicroProse.

[6] The best two recent biographical treatments of Machiavelli in English are Sabastian de Grazia, *Machiavelli in Hell* (New York: Vintage, 1989) (winner of the 1990 Pulitzer Prize for Biography) and Maurizio Viroli, *Niccolò's Smile* (New York: Hill and Wang, 2000).

[7] For an excellent treatment of this milieu, see Peter Godman, *From Polizano to Machiavellli: Florentine Humanism in the High Renaissance* (Princeton: Princeton University Press, 1998).

[8] The letter is often reprinted as a prelude or appendix to English versions of Machiavelli's *The Prince*. I have translated from the original Italian, which may be found in Machiavelli, *Tutte le Opere*, ed. Mario Martelli (Florence: Sansoni, 1971), pp. 1158–1160.

[9] Scholars have disagreed about whether *The Prince*, in the version that has been bequeathed to us, represents a work that Machiavelli polished and added to throughout his life. Thus, for instance, some people have argued the twenty-sixth and final chapter, calling upon the Medici family to unite Italy while driving out the foreign troops housed on Italian soil, constitutes an accretion that reflects later events. The most influential argument in this connection was offered by Hans Baron, "The *Principe* and the Puzzle of the Date of Chapter 26" in *Journal of Medieval and Renaissance Studies*, 21 (1991), pp.83–102. There are, however, many good reasons to believe that the work was conceived and composed as a totality; certainly, its rhetorical development and logical structure are tightly arranged. Whatever editorial grooming Machiavelli performed on the body of his text beyond early 1514 or so was largely cosmetic.

[10] Jean-Jacques Rousseau, *Le contrat sociale*, Book III, Chapter 6.

[11] See Alan Gilbert, *Machiavelli's Prince and Its Forerunners* (Durham, NC: Duke University Press, 1939).

[12] Russell Price, "The Senses of *Virtù* in Machiavelli" in *European Studies Review* 3 (1973), pp.315–345.

[13] Proposed by Mary G. Dietz, "Trapping the Prince: Machiavelli and the Politics of Deception" in *The American Political Science Review*, 80 (1986), pp.777–799.

[14] I rely upon the English translation of the *Discourses* included in Niccolò Machiavelli, *The Chief Works and Others*, ed. and trans. Alan Gilbert, 3 vols. (Durham, NC: Duke University Press, 1965), p.202. (Cited hereafter as *CW*.)

[15] *CW*, p.316.

[16] *CW*, pp.204–205.

[17] *CW*, p.203.

[18] *CW*, p.316.

[19] See Sydney Anglo, *Machiavelli: The First Century* (Oxford: Oxford University Press, 2005).

[20] Maurizio Viroli, *From Politics to Reason of State* (Cambridge: Cambridge University Press, 1992).

[21] Leo Strauss, *Thoughts on Machiavelli* (Glencoe, IL: The Free Press, 1957).

[22] J.G.A. Pocock, *The Machiavellian Moment* (Princeton: Princeton University Press, 1975).

[23] Hans Baron, "Machiavelli: The Republican Citizen and the Author of 'The Prince'" in *The English Historical Review*, 76 (1961), pp.217–253; Quentin Skinner, *The Foundations of Modern Political Thought*, 2 vols. (Cambridge: Cambridge University Press, 1978).

[24] Paul Rahe, *Republicanism—Ancient and Modern* (Chapel Hill: University of North Carolina Press, 1990); Mark Hulliung, *Citizens Machiavelli* (Princeton: Princeton University Press, 1983).

[25] See Janet Coleman, "Machiavelli's *Via Moderna*: Medieval and Renaissance Attitudes to History" in *Niccolò Machiavelli's The Prince: New Interdisciplinary Essays*, ed. Martin Coyle (Manchester: Manchester University Press, 1995), pp.40–64.

THE PRINCE

DEDICATION TO THE MAGNIFICENT LORENZO DI PIERO DE' MEDICI

Those who strive to obtain the good graces of a prince are accustomed to come before him with such things as they hold most precious, or in which they see him take most delight; whence one often sees horses, arms, cloth of gold, precious stones, and similar ornaments presented to princes, worthy of their greatness.

Desiring therefore to present myself to your Magnificence with some testimony of my devotion towards you, I have not found among my possessions anything which I hold more dear than, or value so much as, the knowledge of the actions of great men, acquired by long experience in contemporary affairs, and a continual study of antiquity; which, having reflected upon it with great and prolonged diligence, I now send, digested into a little volume, to your Magnificence.

And although I may consider this work unworthy of your countenance, nevertheless I trust much to your benignity that it may be acceptable, seeing that it is not possible for me to make a better gift than to offer you the opportunity of understanding in the shortest time all that I have learnt in so many years, and with so many troubles and dangers; which work I have not embellished with swelling or magnificent words, nor stuffed with rounded periods, nor with any extrinsic allurements or adornments

whatever, with which so many are accustomed to embellish their works; for I have wished either that no honour should be given it, or else that the truth of the matter and the weightiness of the theme shall make it acceptable.

Nor do I hold with those who regard it as a presumption if a man of low and humble condition dare to discuss and settle the concerns of princes; because, just as those who draw landscapes place themselves below in the plain to contemplate the nature of the mountains and of lofty places, and in order to contemplate the plains place themselves upon high mountains, even so to understand the nature of the people it needs to be a prince, and to understand that of princes it needs to be of the people.

Take then, your Magnificence, this little gift in the spirit in which I send it; wherein, if it be diligently read and considered by you, you will learn my extreme desire that you should attain that greatness which fortune and your other attributes promise. And if your Magnificence from the summit of your greatness will sometimes turn your eyes to these lower regions, you will see how unmeritedly I suffer a great and continued malignity of fortune.

L'ITALIA

Croatia

Sclauonia

Parte d'i Francia

DALFINATO

Prouenza

Mare Hadriaticum siue Superum

GOLFO DI VENETIA

Mare di Genoua

Mare Mediterraneum

MARE TOSCANO

Elba

Isola di Corsica

Epiro

Bocca del Golfo di Venetia

Golfo di Taranto

Mare Ionio

Golfo di Sthilace

Mare Mediterraneum

Isola di Sardigna

Isola di Sicilia

Capo di marsala

Mare Sardo

Isola di San Piero

Mare Mediterraneum

Pachinus p.o

Passaron

CHAPTER I

HOW MANY KINDS OF PRINCIPALITIES THERE ARE, AND BY WHAT MEANS THEY ARE ACQUIRED

ALL STATES, all powers, that have held and hold rule over men have been and are either republics or principalities.

Principalities are either hereditary, in which the family has been long established, or they are new.

The new are either entirely new, as was Milan to Francesco Sforza, or they are, as it were, members annexed to the hereditary state of the prince who has acquired them, as was the kingdom of Naples to that of the king of Spain.

Such dominions thus acquired are either accustomed to live under a prince, or to live in freedom; and are acquired either by the arms of the prince himself, or of others, or else by fortune or by ability.

A map of the states of Italy by Bonsignori and Danti, a wall painting from the Palazzo Vecchio's Sala delle Carte Geografiche, 1575.

CHAPTER II

CONCERNING HEREDITARY PRINCIPALITIES

I WILL leave out all discussion on republics, inasmuch as in another place I have written of them at length, and will address myself only to principalities. In doing so I will keep to the order indicated above, and discuss how such principalities are to be ruled and preserved.

I say at once there are fewer difficulties in holding hereditary states, and those long accustomed to the family of their prince, than new ones; for it is sufficient only not to transgress the customs of his ancestors, and to deal prudently with circumstances as they arise, for a prince of average powers to maintain himself in his state, unless he be deprived of it by some extraordinary and excessive force; and if he should be so deprived of it, whenever anything sinister happens to the usurper, he will regain it.

We have in Italy, for example, the duke of Ferrara, who could not have withstood the attacks of the Venetians in '84, nor those of Pope Julius in '10, unless he had been long established in his dominions. For the hereditary prince has less cause and less necessity to offend; hence it happens that he will be more loved; and unless extraordinary vices cause him to be hated, it is reasonable to expect that his subjects will be naturally well disposed towards him; and in the antiquity and duration of his rule the memories and motives that make for change are lost, for one change always leaves the toothing-stones for another to build upon.

The arms of the House of Este (detail), from Bible des Chartreux by Guglielmo Giraldi, leading Renaissance illuminator to the wealthy.

CHAPTER III

CONCERNING MIXED PRINCIPALITIES

BUT the difficulties occur in a new principality. And firstly, if it be not entirely new, but is, as it were, a member of a state which, taken collectively, may be called composite, the changes arise chiefly from an inherent difficulty which is there in all new principalities; for men change their rulers willingly, hoping to better themselves, and this hope induces them to take up arms against him who rules: wherein they are deceived, because they afterwards find by experience they have gone from bad to worse. This follows also on another natural and common necessity, which always causes a new prince to burden those who have submitted to him with his soldiery and with infinite other hardships which he must put upon his new acquisition.

In this way you have enemies in all those whom you have injured in seizing that principality, and you are not able to keep those friends who put you there because of your not being able to satisfy them in the way they expected, and you cannot take strong measures against them, feeling bound to them. For, although one may be very strong in armed forces, yet in entering a province one has always need of the goodwill of the natives.

For these reasons Louis XII, king of France, quickly occupied Milan, and as quickly lost it; and to turn him out the first time it only needed Lodovico's own forces; because those who had opened the gates to him, finding

King Louis XII in 1503 entering Genoa, ceded earlier by France to the duke of Milan (French manuscript, detail, by Bourdichon).

themselves deceived in their hopes of future benefit, would not endure the ill-treatment of the new prince. It is very true that, after acquiring rebellious provinces a second time, they are not so lightly lost afterwards, because the prince, with little reluctance, takes the opportunity of the rebellion to punish the delinquents, to clear out the suspects, and to strengthen himself in the weakest places. Thus to cause France to lose Milan the first time it was enough for Duke Lodovico to raise insurrections on the borders; but to cause him to lose it a second time it was necessary to bring the whole world against him, and that his armies should be defeated and driven out of Italy; which followed from the causes above mentioned.

Nevertheless Milan was taken from France both the first and the second times. The general reasons for the first have been discussed; it remains to name those for the second, and to see what resources he had, and what any one in his situation would have had for maintaining himself more securely in his acquisition than did the king of France.

Now I say that those dominions which, when acquired, are added to an ancient state by him who acquires them, are either of the same country and language, or they are not. When they are, it is easier to hold them, especially when they have not been accustomed to self-government; and to hold them securely it is enough to have destroyed the family of the prince who was ruling them; because the two peoples, preserving in other things the old conditions, and not being unlike in customs, will live quietly together, as one has seen in Brittany, Burgundy, Gascony, and Normandy, which have been bound to France for so long a time: and, although there may be some difference in language, nevertheless the customs are alike, and the people will easily be able to get on amongst themselves. He who has annexed them,

if he wishes to hold them, has only to bear in mind two considerations: the one, that the family of their former lord is extinguished; the other, that neither their laws nor their taxes are altered, so that in a very short time they will become entirely one body with the old principality.

But when states are acquired in a country differing in language, customs, or laws, there are difficulties, and good fortune and great energy are needed to hold them, and one of the greatest and most real helps would be that he who has acquired them should go and reside there. This would make his position more secure and durable, as it has made that of the Turk in Greece, who, notwithstanding all the other measures taken by him for holding that state, if he had not settled there, would not have been able to keep it. Because, if one is on the spot, disorders are seen as they spring up, and one can quickly remedy them; but if one is not at hand, they are heard of only when they are great, and then one can no longer remedy them. Besides this, the country is not pillaged by your officials; the subjects are satisfied by prompt recourse to the prince; thus, wishing to be good, they have more cause to love him, and wishing to be otherwise, to fear him. He who would attack that state from the outside must have the utmost caution; as long as the prince resides there it can only be wrested from him with the greatest difficulty.

The other and better course is to send colonies to one or two places, which may be as keys to that state, for it is necessary either to do this or else to keep there a great number of cavalry and infantry. A prince does not spend much on colonies, for with little or no expense he can send them out and keep them there, and he offends a minority only of the citizens from whom he takes lands and houses to give them to the new inhabitants; and those whom he offends, remaining poor and scattered, are never able to injure him;

whilst the rest being uninjured are easily kept quiet, and at the same time are anxious not to err for fear it should happen to them as it has to those who have been despoiled. In conclusion, I say that these colonies are not costly, they are more faithful, they injure less, and the injured, as has been said, being poor and scattered, cannot hurt. Upon this, one has to remark that men ought either to be well treated or crushed, because they can avenge themselves of lighter injuries, but of more serious ones they cannot; therefore the injury that is to be done to a man ought to be of such a kind that one does not stand in fear of revenge.

But in maintaining armed men there in place of colonies one spends much more, having to consume on the garrison all income from the state, so that the acquisition turns into a loss, and many more are exasperated, because the whole state is injured; through the shifting of the garrison up and down all become acquainted with hardship, and all become hostile, and they are enemies who, whilst beaten on their own ground, are yet able to do hurt. For every reason, therefore, such guards are as useless as a colony is useful.

Again, the prince who holds a country differing in the above respects ought to make himself the head and defender of his powerful neighbours, and to weaken the more powerful amongst them, taking care that no foreigner as powerful as himself shall, by any accident, get a footing there; for it will always happen that such a one will be introduced by those who are discontented, either through excess of ambition or through fear, as one has seen already. The Romans were brought into Greece by the Aetolians; and in every other country where they obtained a footing they were brought in by the inhabitants. And the usual course of affairs is that, as soon as a powerful foreigner enters a country, all the subject states are drawn to him, moved

by the hatred which they feel against the ruling power. So that in respect to these subject states he has not to take any trouble to gain them over to himself, for the whole of them quickly rally to the state which he has acquired there. He has only to take care that they do not get hold of too much power and too much authority, and then with his own forces, and with their goodwill, he can easily keep down the more powerful of them, so as to remain entirely master in the country. And he who does not properly manage this business will soon lose what he has acquired, and whilst he does hold it he will have endless difficulties and troubles.

The Romans, in the countries which they annexed, observed closely these measures; they sent colonies and maintained friendly relations with the minor powers, without increasing their strength; they kept down the greater, and did not allow any strong foreign powers to gain authority. Greece appears to me sufficient for an example. The Achaeans and Aetolians were kept friendly by them, the kingdom of Macedonia was humbled, Antiochus was driven out; yet the merits of the Achaeans and Aetolians never secured for them permission to increase their power, nor did the persuasions of Philip ever induce the Romans to be his friends without first humbling him, nor did the influence of Antiochus make them agree that he should retain any lordship over the country. Because the Romans did in these instances what all prudent princes ought to do, who have to regard not only present troubles, but also future ones, for which they must prepare with every energy, because, when foreseen, it is easy to remedy them; but if you wait until they approach, the medicine is no longer in time because the malady has become incurable; for it happens in this, as the physicians say it happens in consumption, that in the beginning of the malady it is easy to cure but difficult to detect, but in the course of time, not having been either detected or treated in the beginning, it becomes easy to detect but difficult to cure. Thus it happens in affairs of

state, for when the evils that arise have been foreseen (which it is only given to a wise man to see), they can be quickly redressed, but when, through not having been foreseen, they have been permitted to grow in a way that every one can see them, there is no longer a remedy. Therefore, the Romans, foreseeing troubles, dealt with them at once, and, even to avoid a war, would not let them come to a head, for they knew that war is not to be avoided, but is only put off to the advantage of others; moreover they wished to fight with Philip and Antiochus in Greece so as not to have to do it in Italy; they could have avoided both, but this they did not wish; nor did that ever please them which is forever in the mouths of the wise ones of our time – let us enjoy the benefits of the time – but rather the benefits of their own valour and prudence, for time drives everything before it, and is able to bring with it good as well as evil, and evil as well as good.

But let us turn to France and inquire whether she has done any of the things mentioned. I will speak of Louis [XII] (and not of Charles [VIII]) as the one whose conduct is the better to be observed, he having held possession of Italy for the longest period; and you will see that he has donethe opposite to those things which ought to be done to retain a state composed of divers elements.

King Louis was brought into Italy by the ambition of the Venetians, who desired to obtain half the state of Lombardy by his intervention. I will not blame the course taken by the king, because, wishing to get a foothold in Italy, and having no friends there – seeing rather that every door was shut to him owing to the conduct of Charles – he was forced to accept those friendships which he could get, and he would have succeeded very quickly in his design if in other matters he had not made some mistakes. The king, however, having acquired Lombardy, regained at once the authority which

Charles had lost: Genoa yielded; the Florentines became his friends; the marquess of Mantua, the duke of Ferrara, the Bentivoglio, my lady of Forli, the lords of Faenza, of Pesaro, of Rimini, of Camerino, of Piombino, the Lucchese, the Pisans, the Sienese – everybody made advances to him to become his friend. Then could the Venetians realize the rashness of the course taken by them, which, in order that they might secure two towns in Lombardy, had made the king master of two-thirds of Italy.

Let any one now consider with what little difficulty the king could have maintained his position in Italy had he observed the rules above laid down, and kept all his friends secure and protected; for although they were numerous they were both weak and timid, some afraid of the Church, some of the Venetians, and thus they would always have been forced to stand in with him, and by their means he could easily have made himself secure against those who remained powerful. But he was no sooner in Milan than he did the contrary by assisting Pope Alexander to occupy the Romagna. It never occurred to him that by this action he was weakening himself, depriving himself of friends and those who had thrown themselves into his lap, whilst he aggrandized the Church by adding much temporal power to the spiritual, thus giving it great authority. And having committed this prime error, he was obliged to follow it up, so much so that, to put an end to the ambition of Alexander, and to prevent his becoming the master of Tuscany, he was himself forced to come into Italy.

And as if it were not enough to have aggrandized the Church, and deprived himself of friends, he, wishing to have the kingdom of Naples, divided it with the king of Spain, and where he was the prime arbiter of Italy he takes an associate, so that the ambitious of that country and the malcontents of his

A medallion of Gian Galeazzo Sforza (1469–1494), who became duke of Milan in boyhood but was usurped by his uncle, the regent.

own should have someone to shelter them; and whereas he could have left in the kingdom his own pensioner as king, he drove him out, to put one there who was able to drive him, Louis, out in turn.

The wish to acquire is in truth very natural and common, and men always do so when they can, and for this they will be praised not blamed; but when they cannot do so, yet wish to do so by any means, then there is folly and blame. Therefore, if France could have attacked Naples with her own forces she ought to have done so; if she could not, then she ought not to have divided it. And if the partition which she made with the Venetians in Lombardy was justified by the excuse that by it she got a foothold in Italy, this other partition merited blame, for it had not the excuse of that necessity.

Therefore Louis made these five errors: he destroyed the minor powers, he increased the strength of one of the greater powers in Italy, he brought in a foreign power, he did not settle in the country, he did not send colonies. Which errors, if he had lived, were not enough to injure him had he not made a sixth by taking away their dominions from the Venetians; because, had he not aggrandized the Church, nor brought Spain into Italy, it would have been very reasonable and necessary to humble them; but having first taken these steps, he ought never to have consented to their ruin, for they, being powerful, would always have kept off others from designs on Lombardy, to which the Venetians would never have consented except to become masters themselves there; also because the others would not wish to take Lombardy from France in order to give it to the Venetians, and to run counter to both they would not have had the courage.

And if any one should say: King Louis yielded the Romagna to Alexander and the kingdom to Spain to avoid war, I answer for the reasons given above that a blunder ought never be perpetrated to avoid war, because it is not to be avoided, but is only deferred to your disadvantage. And if another should allege the pledge which the king had given to the Pope that he would assist him in the enterprise, in exchange for the dissolution of his marriage[1] and for making a cardinal of the bishop of Rouen, to that I reply what I shall write later on concerning the faith of princes, and how it ought to be kept.

Thus King Louis lost Lombardy by not having followed any of the conditions observed by those who have taken possession of countries and wished to retain them. Nor is there any miracle in this, but much that is reasonable and quite natural. And on these matters I spoke at Nantes with Rouen, when Valentino,[2] as Cesare Borgia, the son of Pope Alexander, was usually called,

occupied the Romagna, and on Cardinal Rouen[3] observing to me that the Italians did not understand war, I replied to him that the French did not understand statecraft, meaning that otherwise they would not have allowed the Church to reach such greatness. And in fact it has been seen that the greatness of the Church and of Spain in Italy has been caused by France, and her ruin may be attributed to them. From this a general rule is drawn which never or rarely fails: that he who is the cause of another becoming powerful is ruined; because that predominancy has been brought about either by astuteness or else by force, and both are distrusted by him who has been raised to power.

NOTES FOR CHAPTER III

[1] *Louis XII divorced his wife, Jeanne, and married Anne of Britanny, widow of Charles VIII, in 1499, in order to retain the duchy of Britanny.*

[2] *So called – in Italian – from the duchy of Valentinois, conferred on him by Louis XII.*

[3] *The archbishop of Rouen, George d'Amboise, created a cardinal by Alexander VI.*

CHAPTER IV

WHY THE KINGDOM OF DARIUS, CONQUERED BY ALEXANDER,
DID NOT REBEL AGAINST THE SUCCESSORS OF ALEXANDER
AT HIS DEATH

CONSIDERING the difficulties which men have had to hold a newly acquired state, some might wonder how, seeing that Alexander the Great became the master of Asia in a few years, and died whilst it was yet scarcely settled (whence it might appear reasonable that the whole empire would have rebelled), nevertheless his successors maintained themselves, and had to meet no other difficulty than that which arose among themselves from their own ambitions.

I answer that the principalities of which one has record are found to be governed in two different ways: either by a prince, with a body of servants, who assist him to govern the kingdom as ministers by his favour and permission; or by a prince and barons, who hold that dignity by antiquity of blood and not by the grace of the prince. Such barons have states and their own subjects, who recognize them as lords and hold them in natural affection. Those states that are governed by a prince and his servants hold their prince in more consideration, because in all the country there is no one who is recognized as superior to him, and if they yield obedience to another they do it as to a minister and official, and they do not bear him any particular affection.

The examples of these two governments in our time are the Turk and the

*A marble Roman copy of a Greek bust of Alexander the Great, from the
Pinacoteca Capitolina, Rome.*

king of France. The entire monarchy of the Turk is governed by one lord, the others are his servants; and, dividing his kingdom into sanjaks, he sends there different administrators, and shifts and changes them as he chooses. But the king of France is placed in the midst of an ancient body of lords, acknowledged by their own subjects, and beloved by them; they have their

own prerogatives, nor can the king take these away except at his peril. Therefore, he who considers both of these states will recognize great difficulties in seizing the state of the Turk, but, once it is conquered, great ease in holding it. The causes of the difficulties in seizing the kingdom of the Turk are that the usurper cannot be called in by the princes of the kingdom,

nor can he hope to be assisted in his designs by the revolt of those whom the lord has around him. This arises from the reasons given above; for his ministers, being all slaves and bondmen, can only be corrupted with great difficulty, and one can expect little advantage from them when they have been corrupted, as they cannot carry the people with them, for the reasons assigned. Hence, he who attacks the Turk must bear in mind that he will find him united, and he will have to rely more on his own strength than on the revolt of others; but, if once the Turk has been conquered, and routed in the field in such a way that he cannot replace his armies, there is nothing to fear but the family of the prince, and, this being exterminated, there remains no one to fear, the others having no credit with the people; and as the conqueror did not rely on them before his victory, so he ought not to fear them after it.

The contrary happens in kingdoms governed like that of France, because one can easily enter there by gaining over some baron of the kingdom, for one always finds malcontents and such as desire a change. Such men, for the reasons given, can open the way into the state and render the victory easy; but if you wish to hold it afterwards, you meet with infinite difficulties, both from those who have assisted you and from those you have crushed. Nor is it enough for you to have exterminated the family of the prince, because the lords that remain make themselves the heads of fresh movements against you, and as you are unable either to satisfy or exterminate them, that state is lost whenever time brings the opportunity.

(Previous pages) The family of Darius offer obeisance before Alexander after the Battle of Issus, painted by Venetian Paolo Veronese (detail).

Now if you will consider what was the nature of the government of Darius, you will find it similar to the kingdom of the Turk, and therefore it was only necessary for Alexander, first to overthrow him in the field, and then to take the country from him. After which victory, Darius being killed, the state remained secure to Alexander, for the above reasons. And if his successors had been united they would have enjoyed it securely and at their ease, for there were no tumults raised in the kingdom except those they provoked themselves. But it is impossible to hold with such tranquillity states constituted like that of France. Hence arose those frequent rebellions against the Romans in Spain, France, and Greece, owing to the many principalities there were in these states, of which, as long as the memory of them endured, the Romans always held an insecure possession; but with the power and long continuance of the empire the memory of them passed away, and the Romans then became secure possessors. And when fighting afterwards amongst themselves, each one was able to attach to himself his own parts of the country, according to the authority he had assumed there; and the family of the former lord being exterminated, none other than the Romans were acknowledged.

When these things are remembered no one will marvel at the ease with which Alexander held the Empire of Asia, or at the difficulties which others have had to keep an acquisition, such as Pyrrhus and many more; this is not occasioned by the little or abundance of ability in the conqueror, but by the want of uniformity in the subject state.

CHAPTER V

CONCERNING THE WAY TO GOVERN CITIES OR PRINCIPALITIES
WHICH LIVED UNDER THEIR OWN LAWS BEFORE THEY
WERE ANNEXED

WHENEVER those states which have been acquired as stated have been accustomed to live under their own laws and in freedom, there are three courses for those who wish to hold them: the first is to ruin them, the next is to reside there in person, the third is to permit them to live under their own laws, drawing a tribute, and establishing within it an oligarchy which will keep it friendly to you. Because such a government, being created by the prince, knows that it cannot stand without his friendship and interest, and does its utmost to support him; and therefore he who would keep a city accustomed to freedom will hold it more easily by the means of its own citizens than in any other way.

There are, for example, the Spartans and the Romans. The Spartans held Athens and Thebes, establishing there an oligarchy, nevertheless they lost them. The Romans, in order to hold Capua, Carthage, and Numantia, dismantled them, and did not lose them. They wished to hold Greece as the Spartans held it, making it free and permitting its laws, and did not succeed. So to hold it they were compelled to dismantle many cities in the country, for in truth there is no safe way to retain them otherwise than by ruining them. And he who becomes master of a city accustomed to freedom and does not destroy it, may expect to be destroyed by it, for in rebellion it has always the

The Carta della Catena *from 1490 is a panorama of Florence; this detail reveals the Arno, as well as impressive city bridges and walls.*

watch-word of liberty and its ancient privileges as a rallying point, which neither time nor benefits will ever cause it to forget. And whatever you may do or provide against, they never forget that name or their privileges unless they are disunited or dispersed but at every chance they immediately rally to them, as Pisa after the hundred years she had been held in bondage by the Florentines.

But when cities or countries are accustomed to live under a prince, and his family is exterminated, they, being on the one hand accustomed to obey and on the other hand not having the old prince, cannot agree in making one from amongst themselves, and they do not know how to govern themselves. For this reason they are very slow to take up arms, and a prince can gain them to himself and secure them much more easily. But in republics there is more vitality, greater hatred, and more desire for vengeance, which will never permit them to allow the memory of their former liberty to rest; so that the safest way is to destroy them or to reside there.

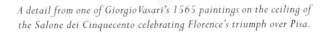

A detail from one of Giorgio Vasari's 1565 paintings on the ceiling of the Salone dei Cinquecento celebrating Florence's triumph over Pisa.

CHAPTER VI

CONCERNING NEW PRINCIPALITIES WHICH ARE ACQUIRED BY
ONE'S OWN ARMS AND ABILITY

LET no one be surprised if, in speaking of entirely new principalities as I shall do, I adduce the highest examples both of prince and of state; because men, walking almost always in paths beaten by others, and following by imitation their deeds, are yet unable to keep entirely to the ways of others or attain to the power of those they imitate. A wise man ought always to follow the paths beaten by great men, and to imitate those who have been supreme, so that if his ability does not equal theirs, at least it will savour of it. Let him act like the clever archers who, designing to hit the mark which yet appears too far distant, and knowing the limits to which the strength of their bow attains, take aim much higher than the mark, not to reach by their strength or arrow to so great a height, but to be able with the aid of so high an aim to hit the mark they wish to reach.

I say, therefore, that in entirely new principalities, where there is a new prince, more or less difficulty is found in keeping them, accordingly as there is more or less ability in him who has acquired the state. Now, as the fact of becoming a prince from a private station presupposes either ability or fortune, it is clear that one or other of these two things will mitigate in some degree many difficulties. Nevertheless, he who has relied least on fortune is established the strongest. Further, it facilitates matters when the prince, having no other state, is compelled to reside there in person.

Duke of Ferrara Alfonso I d'Este (1476–1534; painted by Dossi), who fought successfully to regain his family's fiefdom.

But to come to those who, by their own ability and not through fortune, have risen to be princes, I say that Moses, Cyrus, Romulus, Theseus, and such like are the most excellent examples. And although one may not discuss Moses, he having been a mere executor of the will of God, yet he ought to be admired, if only for that favour which made him worthy to speak with God. But in considering Cyrus and others who have acquired or founded kingdoms, all will be found admirable; and if their particular deeds and conduct shall be considered, they will not be found inferior to those of Moses, although he had so great a preceptor. And in examining their actions and lives one cannot see that they owed anything to fortune beyond opportunity, which brought them the material to mould into the form which seemed best to them. Without that opportunity their powers of mind would have been extinguished, and without those powers the opportunity would have come in vain.

It was necessary, therefore, to Moses that he should find the people of Israel in Egypt enslaved and oppressed by the Egyptians, in order that they should be disposed to follow him so as to be delivered out of bondage. It was necessary that Romulus should not remain in Alba, and that he should be abandoned at his birth, in order that he should become king of Rome and founder of the fatherland. It was necessary that Cyrus should find the Persians discontented with the government of the Medes, and the Medes soft and effeminate through their long peace. Theseus could not have shown his ability had he not found the Athenians dispersed. These opportunities, therefore, made those men fortunate, and their high ability enabled them to recognize the opportunity whereby their country was ennobled and made famous.

Those who by valorous ways become princes, like these men, acquire a principality with difficulty, but they keep it with ease. The difficulties they have

in acquiring it arise in part from the new rules and methods which they are forced to introduce to establish their government and its security. And it ought to be remembered that there is nothing more difficult to take in hand, more perilous to conduct, or more uncertain in its success, than to take the lead in the introduction of a new order of things. Because the innovator has for enemies all those who have done well under the old conditions, and lukewarm defenders in those who may do well under the new. This coolness arises partly from fear of the opponents, who have the laws on their side, and partly from the incredulity of men, who do not readily believe in new things until they have had a long experience of them. Thus it happens that whenever those who are hostile have the opportunity to attack they do it like partisans, whilst the others defend lukewarmly, in such wise that the prince is endangered along with them.

It is necessary, therefore, if we desire to discuss this matter thoroughly, to inquire whether these innovators can rely on themselves or have to depend on others: that is to say, whether, to consummate their enterprise, have they to use prayers or can they use force? In the first instance they always succeed badly, and never accomplish anything; but when they can rely on themselves and use force, then they are rarely endangered. Hence it is that all armed prophets have conquered, and the unarmed ones have been destroyed. Besides the reasons mentioned, the nature of the people is variable, and whilst it is easy to persuade them, it is difficult to fix them in that persuasion. And thus it is necessary to take such measures that, when they believe no longer, it may be possible to make them believe by force.

If Moses, Cyrus, Theseus, and Romulus had been unarmed they could not have enforced their constitutions for long – as happened in our time to Fra

Girolamo Savonarola, who was ruined with his new order of things imme- diately the multitude believed in him no longer, and he had no means of keeping steadfast those who believed or of making the unbelievers to be- lieve. Therefore such as these have great difficulties in consummating their enterprise, for all their dangers are in the ascent, yet with ability they will overcome them; but when these are overcome, and those who envied them their success are exterminated, they will begin to be respected, and they will continue afterwards powerful, secure, honoured, and happy.

To these great examples I wish to add a lesser one; still it bears some resem- blance to them, and I wish it to suffice me for all of a like kind: it is Hiero the Syracusan. This man rose from a private station to be prince of Syracuse, nor did he, either, owe anything to fortune but opportunity; for the Syracusans, being oppressed, chose him for their captain, afterwards he was rewarded by being made their prince. He was of so great ability, even as a private citizen, that one who writes of him says he wanted nothing but a kingdom to be a king. This man abolished the old soldiery, organized the new, gave up old al- liances, made new ones; and as he had his own soldiers and allies, on such foundations he was able to build any edifice: thus, whilst he had endured much trouble in acquiring, he had but little in keeping.

A bronze devotional medallion of Savonarola, created by Luca and Andrea della Robbia, whose family fell under the monk's influence.

CHAPTER VII

CONCERNING NEW PRINCIPALITIES WHICH ARE ACQUIRED EITHER BY THE ARMS OF OTHERS OR BY GOOD FORTUNE

THOSE who solely by good fortune become princes from being private citizens have little trouble in rising, but much in keeping atop; they have not any difficulties on the way up, because they fly, but they have many when they reach the summit. Such are those to whom some state is given either for money or by the favour of him who bestows it; as happened to many in Greece, in the cities of Ionia and of the Hellespont, where princes were made by Darius, in order that they might hold the cities both for his security and his glory; as also were those emperors who, by the corruption of the soldiers, from being citizens came to empire. Such stand simply upon the goodwill and the fortune of him who has elevated them – two most inconstant and unstable things. Neither have they the knowledge requisite for the position; because, unless they are men of great worth and ability, it is not reasonable to expect that they should know how to command, having always lived in a private condition; besides, they cannot hold it because they have not forces which they can keep friendly and faithful.

States that rise unexpectedly, then, like all other things in nature which are born and grow rapidly, cannot have their foundations and relations with other states fixed in such a way that the first storm will not overthrow them; unless, as is said, those who unexpectedly become princes are men of so much ability that they know they have to be prepared at once to hold that which

Pope Alexander VI (detail), a member of the Borgia family who gained notoriety by blatantly promoting the interests of his relatives.

fortune has thrown into their laps, and that those foundations, which others have laid before they became princes, they must lay afterwards.

Concerning these two methods of rising to be a prince by ability or fortune, I wish to adduce two examples within our own recollection, and these are Francesco Sforza[1] and Cesare Borgia. Francesco, by proper means and with great ability, from being a private person rose to be duke of Milan, and that which he had acquired with a thousand anxieties he kept with little trouble. On the other hand, Cesare Borgia, called by the people Duke Valentino, acquired his state during the ascendancy of his father, and on its decline he lost it, notwithstanding that he had taken every measure and done all that ought to be done by a wise and able man to fix firmly his roots in the states which the arms and fortunes of others had bestowed on him.

Because, as is stated above, he who has not first laid his foundations may be able with great ability to lay them afterwards, but they will be laid with trouble to the architect and danger to the building. If, therefore, all the steps taken by the duke be considered, it will be seen that he laid solid foundations for his future power, and I do not consider it superfluous to discuss them, because I do not know what better precepts to give a new prince than the example of his actions; and if his dispositions were of no avail, that was not his fault, but the extraordinary and extreme malignity of fortune.

Alexander VI, in wishing to aggrandize the duke, his son, had many immediate

Cesare Borgia (by Meloni), one of Alexander VI's four children by his mistress — his ambition was met by his father's patronage.

THE ART OF POWER

and prospective difficulties. Firstly, he did not see his way to make him master of any state that was not a state of the Church; and if he was willing to rob the Church he knew that the duke of Milan and the Venetians would not consent, because Faenza and Rimini were already under the protection of the Venetians. Besides this, he saw the arms of Italy, especially those by which he might have been assisted, in hands that would fear the aggrandizement of the Pope, namely, the Orsini and the Colonna and their following. It behoved him, therefore, to upset this state of affairs and embroil the powers, so as to make himself securely master of part of their states. This was easy for him to do, because he found the Venetians, moved by other reasons, inclined to bring back the French into Italy; he would not only not oppose this, but he would render it more easy by dissolving the former marriage of King Louis. Therefore the king came into Italy with the assistance of the Venetians and the consent of Alexander. He was no sooner in Milan than the Pope had soldiers from him for the attempt on the Romagna, which yielded to him on the reputation of the king. The duke, therefore, having acquired the Romagna and beaten the Colonna, while wishing to hold that and to advance further, was hindered by two things: the one, his forces did not appear loyal to him, the other, the goodwill of France; that is to say, he feared that the forces of the Orsini, which he was using, would not stand to him, that not only might they hinder him from winning more, but might themselves seize what he had won, and that the king might also do the same. Of the Orsini he had a warning when, after taking Faenza and attacking Bologna, he saw them go very unwillingly to that attack. And as to the king, he learned his mind when he himself, after taking the duchy of Urbino, attacked Tuscany, and the king made him desist from that undertaking; hence the duke decided to depend no more upon the arms and the luck of others.

For the first thing he weakened the Orsini and Colonna parties in Rome, by

gaining to himself all their adherents who were gentlemen, making them his gentlemen, giving them good pay, and, according to their rank, honouring them with office and command in such a way that in a few months all attachment to the factions was destroyed and turned entirely to the duke. After this he awaited an opportunity to crush the Orsini, having scattered the adherents of the Colonna. This came to him soon and he used it well; for the Orsini, perceiving at length that the aggrandizement of the duke and the Church was ruin to them, called a meeting at Magione, in the territory of Perugia. From this sprung the rebellion at Urbino and the tumults in the Romagna, with endless dangers to the duke, all of which he overcame with the help of the French. Having restored his authority, not to leave it at risk by trusting either to the French or other outside forces, he had recourse to his wiles, and he knew so well how to conceal his mind that, by the mediation of Signor Paolo [Orsini] – whom the duke did not fail to secure with all kinds of attention, giving him money, apparel, and horses – the Orsini were reconciled, so that their simplicity brought them into his power at Sinigaglia. Having exterminated the leaders, and turned their partisans into his friends, the duke had laid sufficiently good foundations to his power, having all the Romagna and the duchy of Urbino; and the people now beginning to appreciate their prosperity, he gained them all over to himself. And as this point is worthy of notice, and to be imitated by others, I am not willing to leave it out.

When the duke occupied the Romagna he found it under the rule of weak masters, who rather plundered their subjects than ruled them, and gave them more cause for disunion than for union, so that the country was full of robbery, quarrels, and every kind of violence; and so, wishing to bring back peace and obedience to authority, he considered it necessary to give it a good governor. Thereupon he promoted Messer Ramiro d'Orco [de Lorqua], a swift and cruel man, to whom he gave the fullest power. This man in a short

time restored peace and unity with the greatest success. Afterwards the duke considered that it was not advisable to confer such excessive authority, for he had no doubt but that he would become odious, so he set up a court of judgment in the country, under a most excellent president, wherein all cities had their advocates. And because he knew that the past severity had caused some hatred against himself, so, to clear himself in the minds of the people, and gain them entirely to himself, he desired to show that, if any cruelty had been practised, it had not originated with him, but in the natural sternness of the minister. Under this pretence he took Ramiro, and one morning caused him to be executed and left on the piazza at Cesena with the block and a bloody knife at his side. The barbarity of this spectacle caused the people to be at once satisfied and dismayed.

But let us return whence we started. I say that the duke, finding himself now sufficiently powerful and partly secured from immediate dangers by having armed himself in his own way, and having in a great measure crushed those forces in his vicinity that could injure him if he wished to proceed with his conquest, had next to consider France, for he knew that the king, who too late was aware of his mistake, would not support him. And from this time he began to seek new alliances and to temporize with France in the expedition which she was making towards the kingdom of Naples against the Spaniards who were besieging Gaeta. It was his intention to secure himself against them, and this he would have quickly accomplished had Alexander lived.

Such was his line of action as to present affairs. But as to the future he had to fear, in the first place, that a new successor to the Church might not be friendly to him and might seek to take from him that which Alexander had given him, so he decided to act in four ways. Firstly, by exterminating the

families of those lords whom he had despoiled, so as to take away that pre-text from the pope. Secondly, by winning to himself all the gentlemen of Rome, so as to be able to curb the pope with their aid, as has been observed. Thirdly, by converting the college more to himself. Fourthly, by acquiring so much power before the pope should die that he could by his own measures resist the first shock. Of these four things, at the death of Alexander, he had accomplished three. For he had killed as many of the dispossessed lords as he could lay hands on, and few had escaped; he had won over the Roman gentlemen, and he had the most numerous party in the college. And as to any fresh acquisition, he intended to become master of Tuscany, for he already possessed Perugia and Piombino, and Pisa was under his protection. And as he had no longer to study France (for the French were already driven out of the kingdom of Naples by the Spaniards, and in this way both were compelled to buy his goodwill), he pounced down upon Pisa. After this, Lucca and Siena yielded at once, partly through hatred and partly through fear of the Florentines; and the Florentines would have had no remedy had he continued to prosper, as he was prospering the year that Alexander died, for he had acquired so much power and reputation that he would have stood by himself, and no longer have depended on the luck and the forces of others, but solely on his own power and ability.

But Alexander died five years after he had first drawn the sword. He left the duke with the state of Romagna alone consolidated, with the rest in the air, between two most powerful hostile armies, and sick unto death. Yet there were in the duke such boldness and ability, and he knew so well how men are to be won or lost, and so firm were the foundations which in so short a time he had laid, that if he had not had those armies on his back, or if he had been in good health, he would have overcome all difficulties. And it is seen that his foundations were good, for the Romagna awaited him for more than a month.

In Rome, although but half alive, he remained secure; and whilst the Baglioni, the Vitelli, and the Orsini might come to Rome, they could not effect anything against him. If he could not have made pope him whom he wished, at least the one whom he did not wish would not have been elected. But if he had been in sound health at the death of Alexander, everything would have been easy to him. On the day that Julius II was elected, he told me that he had thought of everything that might occur at the death of his father, and had provided a remedy for all, except that he had never anticipated that, when the death did happen, he himself would be on the point to die.

When all the actions of the duke are recalled, I do not know how to blame him, but rather it appears to me, as I have said, that I ought to offer him for imitation to all those who, by the fortune or the arms of others, are raised to government. Because he, having a lofty spirit and far-reaching aims, could not have regulated his conduct otherwise, and only the shortness of the life of Alexander and his own sickness frustrated his designs. Therefore, he who considers it necessary to secure himself in his new principality, to win friends, to overcome either by force or fraud, to make himself beloved and feared by the people, to be followed and revered by the soldiers, to exterminate those who have power or reason to hurt him, to change the old order of things for new, to be severe and gracious, magnanimous and liberal, to destroy a disloyal soldiery and to create new, to maintain friendship with kings and princes in such a way that they must help him with zeal and offend with caution, cannot find a more lively example than the actions of this man.

(Previous pages) Urbino cathedral and the Palazzo Ducale, the latter built in the 1460s by the duke, who was commander of papal forces.

THE ART OF POWER

Only can he be blamed for the election of Julius II, in whom he made a bad choice, because, as is said, not being able to elect a pope to his own mind, he could have hindered any other from being elected pope; and he ought never to have consented to the election of any cardinal whom he had injured or who had cause to fear him if they became pontiffs. For men injure either from fear or hatred. Those whom he had injured, amongst others, were San Pietro ad Vincula, Colonna, San Giorgio, and Ascanio.[2] Any one of the others, on becoming pope, would have had to fear him, Rouen and the Spaniards excepted; the latter from their relationship and obligations, the former from his influence, the kingdom of France having relations with him. Therefore, above everything, the duke ought to have created a Spaniard pope, and, failing him, he ought to have consented to Rouen and not San Pietro ad Vincula. He who believes that new benefits will cause great personages to forget old injuries is deceived. Therefore, the duke erred in his choice, and it was the cause of his ultimate ruin.

NOTES FOR CHAPTER VII

[1] *Francesco Sforza married Bianca Maria Visconti, daughter of Filippo Visconti, duke of Milan, on whose death he procured his own elevation to the duchy.*

[2] *Julius II, Giuliano della Rovere, had been cardinal of San Pietro ad Vincula; San Giorgio was Raffaello Riario, and Ascanio was Ascanio Sforza.*

CHAPTER VIII

CONCERNING THOSE WHO HAVE OBTAINED A PRINCIPALITY BY WICKEDNESS

ALTHOUGH a prince may rise from a private station in two ways, neither of which can be entirely attributed to fortune or genius, yet it is manifest to me that I must not be silent on them, although one could be more copiously treated when I discuss republics. These methods are when, either by some wicked or nefarious ways, one ascends to the principality, or when by the favour of his fellow-citizens a private person becomes the prince of his country. And speaking of the first method, it will be illustrated by two examples – one ancient, the other modern – and without entering further into the subject, I consider these two examples will suffice those who may be compelled to follow them.

Agathocles, the Sicilian, became king of Syracuse not only from a private but from a low and abject position. This man, the son of a potter, through all the changes in his fortunes always led an infamous life. Nevertheless, he accompanied his infamies with so much ability of mind and body that, having devoted himself to the military profession, he rose through its ranks to be praetor of Syracuse. Being established in that position, and having deliberately resolved to make himself prince and to seize by violence, without obligation to others, that which had been conceded to him by assent, he came to an understanding for this purpose with Hamilcar, the Carthaginian, who, with his army, was fighting in Sicily. One morning he assembled the people and senate

The Massacre of the Innocents *(detail) in Siena's Palazzo Pubblico is a disturbing work, warning of cruel deeds by the powerful.*

of Syracuse, as if he had to discuss with them things relating to the republic, and at a given signal the soldiers killed all the senators and the richest of the people; these dead, he seized and held the princedom of that city without any civil commotion. And although he was twice routed by the Carthaginians, and ultimately besieged, yet not only was he able to defend his city, but leaving part of his men for its defence, with the others he attacked Africa, and in a short time raised the siege of Syracuse. The Carthaginians, reduced to extreme necessity, were compelled to come to terms with Agathocles, and, leaving Sicily to him, had to be content with the possession of Africa.

Therefore, he who considers the actions and the genius of this man will see nothing, or little, which can be attributed to fortune, inasmuch as he attained pre-eminence, as is shown above, not by the favour of any one, but step by step in the military profession, which steps were gained with a thousand troubles and perils, and were afterwards boldly held by him with many hazards and dangers. Yet it cannot be called virtue to slay fellow-citizens, to deceive friends, to be without faith, without mercy, without religion; such methods may gain empire, but not glory. Still, if the courage of Agathocles in entering into and extricating himself from dangers be considered, together with his greatness of mind in enduring overcoming hardships, it cannot be seen why he should be esteemed less than the most notable captain. Nevertheless, his barbarous cruelty and inhumanity with infinite wickednesses do not permit him to be celebrated among the most excellent men. What he achieved cannot be attributed either to fortune or to genius.

In our times, during the rule of Alexander VI, Oliverotto da Fermo, having been left an orphan many years before, was brought up by his maternal uncle, Giovanni Fogliani, and in the early days of his youth sent to fight under

Paolo Vitelli, that, being trained under his discipline, he might attain some high position in the military profession. After Paolo died, he fought under his brother Vitellozzo, and in a very short time, being endowed with wit and a vigorous body and mind, he became the first man in his profession. But it appearing to him a paltry thing to serve under others, he resolved, with the aid of some citizens of Fermo, to whom the slavery of their country was dearer than its liberty, and with the help of the Vitelli, to seize Fermo. So he wrote to Giovanni Fogliani that, having been away from home for many years, he wished to visit him and his city, and in some measure to look into his patrimony; and although he had not laboured to acquire anything except honour, yet, in order that the citizens should see he had not spent his time in vain, he desired to come honourably, so would be accompanied by one hundred horsemen, his friends and retainers; and he entreated Giovanni to arrange that he should be received honourably by the citizens of Fermo, all of which would be not only to his honour, but also to that of Giovanni himself, who had brought him up.

Giovanni, therefore, did not fail in any attentions due to his nephew, and he caused him to be honourably received by the Fermans, and he lodged him in his own house, where, having passed some days, and having arranged what was necessary for his wicked designs, Oliverotto gave a solemn banquet to which he invited Giovanni Fogliani and the chiefs of Fermo. When the viands and all the other entertainments that are usual in such banquets were finished, Oliverotto artfully began certain grave discourses, speaking of the greatness of Pope Alexander and his son Cesare, and of their enterprises, to which discourse Giovanni and others answered; but he rose at once, saying that such matters ought to be discussed in a more private place, and he betook himself to a chamber, whither Giovanni and the rest of the citizens went in after him. No sooner were they seated than soldiers issued from

secret places and slaughtered Giovanni and the rest. After these murders
Oliverotto, mounted on horseback, rode up and down the town and besieged
the chief magistrate in the palace, so that in fear the people were forced to
obey him, and to form a government, of which he made himself the prince.
He killed all the malcontents who were able to injure him, and strengthened
himself with new civil and military ordinances, in such a way that, in the year
during which he held the principality, not only was he secure in the city of
Fermo, but he had become formidable to all his neighbours. And his destruction would have been as difficult as that of Agathocles if he had not allowed
himself to be overreached by Cesare Borgia, who took him with the Orsini
and Vitelli at Sinigaglia, as was stated above. Thus one year after he had committed this parricide, he was strangled, together with Vitellozzo, whom he
had made his leader in valour and wickedness.

Some may wonder how it can happen that Agathocles, and his like, after infinite treacheries and cruelties, should live for long secure in his country, and
defend himself from external enemies, and never be conspired against by his
own citizens; seeing that many others, by means of cruelty, have never been
able even in peaceful times to hold the state, still less in the doubtful times of
war. I believe that this follows from severities being badly or properly used.
Those may be called properly used, if of evil it is lawful to speak well, that
are applied at one blow and are necessary to one's security, and that are not
persisted in afterwards unless they can be turned to the advantage of the subjects. The badly employed are those which, notwithstanding they may be few
in the commencement, multiply with time rather than decrease. Those who
practise the first system are able, by aid of God or man, to mitigate in some

*(Previous pages) In 1328 the Gonzaga family overthrew and expelled
the Bonacolsi dynasty in Mantua, depicted here by Morone in 1494.*

degree their rule, as Agathocles did. It is impossible for those who follow the other to maintain themselves.

Hence it is to be remarked that, in seizing a state, the usurper ought to examine closely into all those injuries which it is necessary for him to inflict, and to do them all at one stroke so as not to have to repeat them daily; and thus by not unsettling men he will be able to reassure them, and win them to himself by benefits. He who does otherwise, either from timidity or evil advice, is always compelled to keep the knife in his hand; neither can he rely on his subjects, nor can they attach themselves to him, owing to their continued and repeated wrongs. For injuries ought to be done all at one time, so that, being tasted less, they offend less; benefits ought to be given little by little, so that the flavour of them may last longer.

And above all things, a prince ought to live amongst his people in such a way that no unexpected circumstances, whether of good or evil, shall make him change; because if the necessity for this comes in troubled times, you are too late for harsh measures; and mild ones will not help you, for they will be considered as forced from you, and no one will be under any obligation to you for them.

MAGNAN

CHAPTER IX

CONCERNING A CIVIL PRINCIPALITY

BUT coming to the other point – where a leading citizen becomes the prince of his country, not by wickedness or any intolerable violence, but by the favour of his fellow citizens – this may be called a civil principality: nor is genius or fortune altogether necessary to attain to it, but rather a happy shrewdness. I say then that such a principality is obtained either by the favour of the people or by the favour of the nobles. Because in all cities these two distinct parties are found, and from this it arises that the people do not wish to be ruled nor oppressed by the nobles, and the nobles wish to rule and oppress the people; and from these two opposite desires there arises in cities one of three results, either a principality, self-government, or anarchy.

A principality is created either by the people or by the nobles, accordingly as one or other of them has the opportunity; for the nobles, seeing they cannot withstand the people, begin to cry up the reputation of one of themselves, and they make him a prince, so that under his shadow they can give vent to their ambitions. The people, finding they cannot resist the nobles, also cry up the reputation of one of themselves, and make him a prince so as to be defended by his authority. He who obtains sovereignty by the assistance of the nobles maintains himself with more difficulty than he who comes to it by the aid of the people, because the former finds himself with many around him who consider themselves his equals, and because of this he can neither rule nor manage them to his liking. But he who reaches sovereignty by popular favour finds himself

The just ruler in Allegory of Good Government *(1338–1340; detail) by Lorenzetti, a fresco in Siena's Hall of the Nine.*

alone, and has none around him, or few, who are not prepared to obey him. Besides this, one cannot by fair dealing, and without injury to others, satisfy the nobles, but you can satisfy the people, for their object is more righteous than that of the nobles, the latter wishing to oppress, whilst the former only desire not to be oppressed. It is to be added also that a prince can never secure himself against a hostile people, because of their being too many, whilst from the nobles he can secure himself, as they are few in number. The worst that a prince may expect from a hostile people is to be abandoned by them; but from hostile nobles he has not only to fear abandonment, but also that they will rise against him; for they, being in these affairs more far-seeing and astute, always come forward in time to save themselves, and to obtain favours from him whom they expect to prevail. Further, the prince is compelled to live always with the same people, but he can do well without the same nobles, being able to make and unmake them daily, and to give or take away authority when it pleases him.

Therefore, to make this point clearer, I say that the nobles ought to be looked at mainly in two ways: that is to say, they either shape their course in such a way as binds them entirely to your fortune, or they do not. Those who so bind themselves, and are not rapacious, ought to be honoured and loved; those who do not bind themselves may be dealt with in two ways; they may fail to do this through pusillanimity and a natural want of courage, in which case you ought to make use of them, especially of those who are of good counsel; and thus, whilst in prosperity you honour yourself, in adversity you have not to fear them. But when for their own ambitious ends they shun binding themselves, it is a token that they are giving more thought to themselves than to you, and a prince ought to guard against such, and to fear them as if they were open enemies, because in adversity they always help to ruin him. Therefore, one who becomes a prince through the favour of the people ought

to keep them friendly, and this he can easily do seeing they only ask not to be oppressed by him. But one who, in opposition to the people, becomes a prince by the favour of the nobles, ought, above everything, to seek to win the people over to himself, and this he may easily do if he takes them under his protection. Because men, when they receive good from him of whom they were expecting evil, are bound more closely to their benefactor; thus the people quickly become more devoted to him than if he had been raised to the principality by their favours; and the prince can win their affections in many ways, but as these vary according to the circumstances one cannot give fixed rules, so I omit them; but, I repeat, it is necessary for a prince to have the people friendly, otherwise he has no security in adversity.

Nabis, prince of the Spartans, sustained the attack of all Greece, and of a victorious Roman army, and against them he defended his country and his government; and for the overcoming of this peril it was only necessary for him to make himself secure against a few, but this would not have been sufficient if the people had been hostile. And do not let any one impugn this statement with the trite proverb that "He who builds on the people, builds on the mud", for this is true when a private citizen makes a foundation there, and persuades himself that the people will free him when he is oppressed by his enemies or by the magistrates; wherein he would find himself very often deceived, as happened to the Gracchi in Rome and to Messer Giorgio Scali in Florence. But granted a prince who has established himself as above, who can command, and is a man of courage, undismayed in adversity, who does not fail in other qualifications, and who, by his reso-lution and energy, keeps the whole people encouraged – such a one will never find himself deceived in them, and it will be shown that he has laid his foundations well.

These principalities are liable to danger when they are passing from the civil to the absolute order of government, for such princes either rule personally or through magistrates. In the latter case their government is weaker and more insecure, because it rests entirely on the goodwill of those citizens who are raised to the magistracy, and who, especially in troubled times, can destroy the government with great ease, either by intrigue or open defiance; and the prince has not the chance amid tumults to exercise absolute authority, because the citizens and subjects, accustomed to receive orders from magistrates, are not of a mind to obey him amid these confusions, and there will always be in doubtful times a scarcity of men whom he can trust. For such a prince cannot rely upon what he observes in quiet times, when citizens had need of the state, because then every one agrees with him; they all promise, and when death is far distant they all wish to die for him; but in

troubled times, when the state has need of its citizens, then he finds but few. And so much the more is this experiment dangerous, inasmuch as it can only be tried once. Therefore a wise prince ought to adopt such a course that his citizens will always in every sort and kind of circumstance have need of the state and of him, and then he will always find them faithful.

The Ideal City, *thought to have been painted by Piero della Francesca (ca. 1470), symbolizes peace, balance and orderly rhythm.*

CHAPTER X

CONCERNING THE WAY IN WHICH THE STRENGTH OF ALL PRINCIPALITIES OUGHT TO BE MEASURED

IT IS necessary to consider another point in examining the character of these principalities: that is, whether a prince has such power that, in case of need, he can support himself with his own resources, or whether he has always need of the assistance of others. And to make this quite clear I say that I consider those are able to support themselves by their own resources who can, either by abundance of men or money, raise a sufficient army to join battle against any one who comes to attack them; and I consider those always to have need of others who cannot show themselves against the enemy in the field, but are forced to defend themselves by sheltering behind walls. The first case has been discussed, but we will speak of it again should it recur. In the second case one can say nothing except to encourage such princes to provision and fortify their towns, and not on any account to defend the country. And whoever shall fortify his town well, and shall have managed the other concerns of his subjects in the way stated above, and to be often repeated, will never be attacked without great caution, for men are always adverse to enterprises where difficulties can be seen, and it will be seen not to be an easy thing to attack one who has his town well fortified, and is not hated by his people.

The cities of Germany are absolutely free, they own but little country around them, and they yield obedience to the emperor when it suits them, nor do they fear this or any other power they may have near them, because they

---

Erasmo of Narni, better known as Gattamelata ("The Honeyed Cat"), was a famous mercenary who served the papacy, Florence and Venice.

are fortified in such a way that everyone thinks the taking of them by assault would be tedious and difficult, seeing they have proper ditches and walls, they have sufficient artillery, and they always keep in public depots enough for one year's eating, drinking, and firing. And beyond this, to keep the people quiet and without loss to the state, they always have the means of giving work to the community in those labours that are the life and strength of the city, and on the pursuit of which the people are supported; they also hold military exercises in repute, and moreover have many ordinances to uphold them.

Therefore, a prince who has a strong city, and has not made himself odious, will not be attacked, or if any one should attack he will only be driven off with disgrace; again, because the affairs of this world are so changeable, it is almost impossible to keep an army a whole year in the field without being interfered with. And whoever should reply: If the people have property outside the city, and see it burnt, they will not remain patient, and the long siege and self-interest will make them forget their prince; to this I answer that a powerful and courageous prince will overcome all such difficulties by giving at one time hope to his subjects that the evil will not be for long, at another time fear of the cruelty of the enemy, then preserving himself adroitly from those subjects who seem to him to be too bold.

Further, the enemy would naturally on his arrival at once burn and ruin the country at the time when the spirits of the people are still hot and ready for the defence; and, therefore, so much the less ought the prince to hesitate; because after a time, when spirits have cooled, the damage is already done, the ills are incurred, and there is no longer any remedy; and therefore they are so much the more ready to unite with their prince, he appearing to be

under obligations to them now that their houses have been burnt and their possessions ruined in his defence. For it is the nature of men to be bound by the benefits they confer as much as by those they receive. Therefore, if everything is well considered, it will not be difficult for a wise prince to keep the minds of his citizens steadfast from first to last, when he does not fail to support and defend them.

CHAPTER XI

CONCERNING ECCLESIASTICAL PRINCIPALITIES

IT ONLY remains now to speak of ecclesiastical principalities, touching which all difficulties are prior to getting possession, because they are acquired either by capacity or good fortune, and they can be held without either; for they are sustained by the ordinances of religion, which are so all-powerful, and of such a character that the principalities may be held no matter how their princes behave and live. These princes alone have states and do not defend them, they have subjects and do not rule them; and the states, although unguarded, are not taken from them; and the subjects, although not ruled, do not care, and they have neither the desire nor the ability to alienate themselves. Such principalities only are secure and happy. But being upheld by powers, to which the human mind cannot reach, I shall speak no more of them, because, being exalted and maintained by God, it would be the act of a presumptuous and rash man to discuss them.

Nevertheless, if any one should ask of me how comes it that the Church has attained such greatness in temporal power, seeing that from Alexander backwards the Italian potentates (not only those who have been called potentates, but every baron and lord, though the smallest) have valued the temporal power very slightly – yet now a king of France trembles before it, and it has been able to drive him from Italy, and to ruin the Venetians – although this may be very manifest, it does not appear to me superfluous to recall it in some measure to memory.

The papal arms decorate the stair pier at the Duomo in Todi, Umbria.
The city was annexed by the papal states in the 14th century.

Before Charles, king of France, passed into Italy, this country was under the dominion of the pope, the Venetians, the king of Naples, the duke of Milan, and the Florentines. These potentates had two principal anxieties: the one, that no foreigner should enter Italy under arms; the other, that none of themselves should seize more territory. Those about whom there was the most anxiety were the pope and the Venetians. To restrain the Venetians the union of all the others was necessary, as it was for the defence of Ferrara; and to keep down the pope they made use of the barons of Rome, who, being divided into two factions, Orsini and Colonna, had always a pretext for disorder, and, standing with arms in their hands under the eyes of the pontiff, kept the pontificate weak and powerless. And although there might arise sometimes a courageous pope, such as Sixtus [IV], yet neither fortune nor wisdom could rid him of these annoyances. And the short life of a pope is also a cause of weakness; for in the ten years, which is the average life of a pope, he can with difficulty lower one of the factions; and if, so to speak, one pope should almost destroy the Colonna, another would arise hostile to the Orsini, who would support their opponents, and yet would not have time to ruin the Orsini. This was the reason why the temporal powers of the pope were little esteemed in Italy.

Alexander VI arose afterwards, who of all the pontiffs that have ever been showed how a pope with both money and arms was able to prevail; and through the instrumentality of Duke Valentino, and by reason of the entry of the French, he brought about all those things which I have discussed above in the actions of the duke. And although his intention was not to aggrandize the Church, but the duke, nevertheless, what he did contributed to the greatness

Renaissance armour was often a visual feast. Gaspare Mola made this helmet, adorned with ancient and mythical motifs.

THE ART OF POWER

THE ART OF POWER

of the Church, which, after his death and the ruin of the duke, became the heir to all his labours.

Pope Julius came afterwards and found the Church strong, possessing all the Romagna, the barons of Rome reduced to impotence, and, through the chastisements of Alexander, the factions wiped out; he also found the way open to accumulate money in a manner such as had never been practised before Alexander's time. Such things Julius not only followed, but improved upon, and he intended to gain Bologna, to ruin the Venetians, and to drive the French out of Italy. All of these enterprises prospered with him, and so much the more to his credit, inasmuch as he did everything to strengthen the Church and not any private person. He kept also the Orsini and Colonna factions within the bounds in which he found them; and although there was among them some mind to make disturbance, nevertheless he held two things firm: the one, the greatness of the Church, with which he terrified them; and the other, not allowing them to have their own cardinals, who caused the disorders among them. For whenever these factions have their cardinals they do not remain quiet for long, because cardinals foster the factions in Rome and out of it, and the barons are compelled to support them, and thus from the ambitions of prelates arise disorders and tumults among the barons. For these reasons his Holiness Pope Leo found the pontificate most powerful, and it is to be hoped that, if others made it great in arms, he will make it still greater and more venerated by his goodness and infinite other virtues.

Departure of the English Ambassadors (1498; detail, by Vittorio Carpaccio) from Venice, a city which began life as an episcopal see.

CHAPTER XII

HOW MANY KINDS OF SOLDIERY THERE ARE,
AND CONCERNING MERCENARIES

HAVING discoursed particularly on the characteristics of such principalities as in the beginning I proposed to discuss, and having considered in some degree the causes of their being good or bad, and having shown the methods by which many have sought to acquire them and to hold them, it now remains for me to discuss generally the means of offence and defence which belong to each of them.

We have seen above how necessary it is for a prince to have his foundations well laid, otherwise it follows of necessity he will go to ruin. The chief foundations of all states, new as well as old or composite, are good laws and good arms; and as there cannot be good laws where the state is not well armed, it follows that where they are well armed they have good laws. I shall leave the laws out of the discussion and shall speak of the arms.

I say, therefore, that the arms with which a prince defends his state are either his own, or they are mercenaries, auxiliaries, or mixed. Mercenaries and auxiliaries are useless and dangerous; and if one holds his state based on these arms, he will stand neither firm nor safe; for they are disunited, ambitious and without discipline, unfaithful, valiant before friends, cowardly before enemies; they have neither the fear of God nor fidelity to men, and

---

Sir John Hawkwood, an English mercenary known as Giovanni Acuto, who served most sides over 30 years; fresco by Paolo Uccello (1436).

destruction is deferred only so long as the attack is; for in peace one is robbed by them, and in war by the enemy. The fact is, they have no other attraction or reason for keeping the field than a trifle of stipend, which is not sufficient to make them willing to die for you. They are ready enough to be your soldiers whilst you do not make war, but if war comes they take themselves off or run from the foe; which I should have little trouble to prove, for the ruin of Italy has been caused by nothing else than by resting all her hopes for many years on mercenaries, and although they formerly made some display and appeared valiant amongst themselves, yet when the foreigners came they showed what they were. Thus it was that Charles, king of France, was allowed to seize Italy with chalk in hand;[1] and he who told us that our sins were the cause of it told the truth, but they were not the sins he imagined, but those which I have related. And as they were the sins of princes, it is the princes who have also suffered the penalty.

I wish to demonstrate further the infelicity of these arms. The mercenary captains are either capable men or they are not; if they are, you cannot trust them, because they always aspire to their own greatness, either by oppressing you, who are their master, or others contrary to your intentions; but if the captain is not skilful, you are ruined in the usual way.

And if it be urged that whoever is armed will act in the same way, whether mercenary or not, I reply that when arms have to be resorted to, either by a prince or a republic, then the prince ought to go in person and perform the duty of captain; the republic has to send its citizens, and when one is sent who does not turn out satisfactorily, it ought to recall him, and when one is worthy, to hold him by the laws so that he does not leave the command. And experience has shown princes and republics, single-handed, making the

THE ART OF POWER

greatest progress, and mercenaries doing nothing except damage; and it is more difficult to bring a republic, armed with its own arms, under the sway of one of its citizens than it is to bring one armed with foreign arms. Rome and Sparta stood for many ages armed and free. The Switzers are completely armed and quite free.

Of ancient mercenaries, for example, there are the Carthaginians, who were oppressed by their mercenary soldiers after the first war with the Romans, although the Carthaginians had their own citizens for captains. After the death of Epaminondas, Philip of Macedon was made captain of their soldiers by the Thebans, and after victory he took away their liberty.

Duke Filippo being dead, the Milanese enlisted Francesco Sforza against the Venetians, and he, having overcome the enemy at Caravaggio, allied himself with them to crush the Milanese, his masters. His father, Sforza, having been engaged by Queen Johanna of Naples, left her unprotected, so that she was forced to throw herself into the arms of the king of Aragon, in order to save her kingdom. And if the Venetians and Florentines formerly extended their dominions by these arms, and yet their captains did not make themselves princes, but have defended them, I reply that the Florentines in this case have been favoured by chance, for of the able captains, of whom they might have stood in fear, some have not conquered, some have been opposed, and others have turned their ambitions elsewhere. One who did not conquer was Giovanni Acuto,[2] and since he did not conquer his fidelity cannot be proved; but everyone will acknowledge that, had he conquered, the Florentines would have stood at his discretion. Sforza had the Bracceschi always against him, so they watched each other. Francesco turned his ambition to Lombardy; Braccio against the Church and the kingdom of Naples. But let us come to

that which happened a short while ago. The Florentines appointed as their captain Paolo Vitelli, a most prudent man, who from a private position had risen to the greatest renown. If this man had taken Pisa, nobody can deny that it would have been proper for the Florentines to keep in with him, for if he became the soldier of their enemies they had no means of resisting, and if they held to him they must obey him. The Venetians, if their achievements are considered, will be seen to have acted safely and gloriously so long as they sent to war their own men, when with armed gentlemen and plebeians they

did valiantly. This was before they turned to enterprises on land, but when they began to fight on land they forsook this virtue and followed the custom of Italy. And in the beginning of their expansion on land, through not having much territory, and because of their great reputation, they had not much to fear from their captains; but when they expanded, as under Carmignola, they had a taste of this mistake; for, having found him a most valiant man (they beat the duke of Milan under his leadership), and, on the other hand, knowing how lukewarm he was in the war, they feared they would no longer

conquer under him, and for this reason they were not willing, nor were they able, to let him go; and so, not to lose again that which they had acquired, they were compelled, in order to secure themselves, to murder him. They had afterwards for their captains Bartolomeo da Bergamo, Roberto da San Severino, the count of Pitigliano, and the like, under whom they had to dread loss and not gain, as happened afterwards at Vaila, where in one battle they lost that which in eight hundred years they had acquired with so much trouble. Because from such arms conquests come but slowly, long delayed and inconsiderable, but the losses sudden and portentous.

And as with these examples I have reached Italy, which has been ruled for many years by mercenaries, I wish to discuss them more seriously, in order that, having seen their rise and progress, one may be better prepared to counteract them. You must understand that the empire has recently come to be repudiated in Italy, that the pope has acquired more temporal power, and that Italy has been divided up into more states, for the reason that many of the great cities took up arms against their nobles, who, formerly favoured by the emperor, were oppressing them, whilst the Church was favouring them so as to gain authority in temporal power: in many others their citizens became princes. From this it came to pass that Italy fell partly into the hands of the Church and of republics, and, the Church consisting of priests and the republic of citizens unaccustomed to arms, both commenced to enlist foreigners.

The first who gave renown to this soldiery was Alberigo da Conio, a native of the Romagna. From the school of this man sprang, among others, Braccio and

(Previous pages) A painting (detail) by Paolo Uccello of The Battle of San Romano, *fought between Florence and Siena in 1432.*

THE ART OF POWER

Sforza, who in their time were the arbiters of Italy. After these came all the other captains who till now have directed the arms of Italy; and the end of all their valour has been, that she has been overrun by Charles, robbed by Louis, ravaged by Ferdinand, and insulted by the Switzers. The principle that has guided them has been, first, to lower the credit of infantry so that they might increase their own. They did this because, subsisting on their pay and without territory, they were unable to support many soldiers, and a few infantry did not give them any authority; so they were led to employ cavalry, with a moderate force of which they were maintained and honoured; and affairs were brought to such a pass that, in an army of twenty thousand soldiers, there were not to be found two thousand foot soldiers. They had, besides this, used every art to lessen fatigue and danger to themselves and their soldiers, not killing in the fray, but taking prisoners and liberating without ransom. They did not attack towns at night, nor did the garrisons of the towns attack encampments at night; they did not surround the camp either with stockade or ditch, nor did they campaign in the winter. All these things were permitted by their military rules, and devised by them to avoid, as I have said, both fatigue and dangers; thus they have brought Italy to slavery and contempt.

NOTES FOR CHAPTER XII

[1] *With which to chalk up the billets for his soldiers. From "col gesso", one of the* bon mots *of Alexander VI, referring to the ease with which Charles VIII seized Italy, implying that it was only necessary for him to send his quartermasters to chalk up the billets for his soldiers to conquer the country.*

[2] *As Sir John Hawkwood, the English leader of mercenaries, was called by the Italians. He fought in England's wars in France and was knighted by Edward III. Afterwards he gathered a body of troops and went to Italy. His force became the famous "White Company" and took part in many battles. Born in Essex in about 1320, he died in Florence in 1394, having married Domnia, a daughter of Bernabo Visconti.*

CHAPTER XIII

CONCERNING AUXILIARIES, MIXED SOLDIERY, AND ONE'S OWN

AUXILIARIES, which are the other useless arm, are employed when a prince is called in with his forces to aid and defend, as was done by Pope Julius in the most recent times; for he, having, in the enterprise against Ferrara, had poor proof of his mercenaries, turned to auxiliaries, and stipulated with Ferdinand, king of Spain, for his assistance with men and arms. These arms may be useful and good in themselves, but for him who calls them in they are always disadvantageous; for losing, one is undone, and winning, one is their captive.

And although ancient histories may be full of examples, I do not wish to leave this recent one of Pope Julius II, the peril of which cannot fail to be perceived; for he, wishing to get Ferrara, threw himself entirely into the hands of the foreigner. But his good fortune brought about a third event, so that he did not reap the fruit of his rash choice; because, having auxiliaries routed at Ravenna, and the Switzers having risen and driven out the conquerors (against all expectation, both his and others), it so came to pass that he did not become prisoner to his enemies, they having fled, nor to his auxiliaries, he having conquered by other arms than theirs.

The Florentines, being entirely without arms, sent ten thousand Frenchmen to take Pisa, whereby they ran into more danger than at any other time of their troubles. The emperor of Constantinople, to oppose his neighbours, sent ten

The Battle of Pavia *(detail) in 1525 marked the beginning of the Lombardy city's domination by foreign powers for several centuries.*

thousand Turks into Greece, who, on the war being finished, were not willing to quit; this was the beginning of the servitude of Greece to the infidels.

Therefore, let him who has no desire to conquer make use of these arms, for they are much more hazardous than mercenaries, because with them the ruin is ready made; they are all united, all yield obedience to others; but with mercenaries, when they have conquered, more time and better opportunities are needed to injure you; they are not all of one community, they are found and paid by you, and a third party, which you have made their head, is not able all at once to assume enough authority to injure you. In conclusion, in mercenaries dastardy is most dangerous; in auxiliaries, valour. The wise prince, therefore, has always avoided these arms and turned to his own; and has been willing rather to lose with them than to conquer with others, not deeming that a real victory which is gained with the arms of others.

I shall never hesitate to cite Cesare Borgia and his actions. This duke entered the Romagna with auxiliaries, taking there only French soldiers, and with them he captured Imola and Forli; but afterwards, such forces not appearing to him reliable, he turned to mercenaries, discerning less danger in them, and enlisted the Orsini and Vitelli; whom presently, on handling and finding them doubtful, unfaithful, and dangerous, he destroyed and turned to his own men. And the difference between one and the other of these forces can easily be seen when one considers the difference there was in the reputation of the duke, when he had the French, when he had the Orsini and Vitelli, and when he relied on his own soldiers, on whose fidelity he could always count and

David the Israelite beheads the Philistine Goliath in a lower panel of Lorenzo Ghiberti's Doors of Paradise at the Baptistery in Florence.

THE ART OF POWER

found it ever increasing; he was never esteemed more highly than when every one saw that he was complete master of his own forces.

I was not intending to go beyond Italian and recent examples, but I am unwilling to leave out Hiero, the Syracusan, he being one of those I have named above. This man, as I have said, made head of the army by the Syracusans, soon found out that a mercenary soldiery, constituted like our Italian condottieri, was of no use; and it appearing to him that he could neither keep them nor let them go, he had them all cut to pieces, and afterwards made war with his own forces and not with aliens.

I wish also to recall to memory an instance from the Old Testament applicable to this subject. David offered himself to Saul to fight with Goliath, the Philistine champion, and, to give him courage, Saul armed him with his own weapons; which David rejected as soon as he had them on his back, saying he could make no use of them, and that he wished to meet the enemy with his sling and his knife. In conclusion, the arms of others either fall from your back, or they weigh you down, or they bind you fast.

Charles VII, the father of King Louis XI, having by good fortune and valour liberated France from the English, recognized the necessity of being armed with forces of his own, and he established in his kingdom ordinances concerning men-at-arms and infantry. Afterwards his son, King Louis, abolished the infantry and began to enlist the Switzers, which mistake, followed by others,

Charles VII of France, the Valois monarch who united most of the country and created a standing army, portrait by Fouquet.

is, as is now seen, a source of peril to that kingdom; because, having raised the reputation of the Switzers, he has entirely diminished the value of his own arms, for he has destroyed the infantry altogether; and his men-at-arms he has subordinated to others, for, being as they are so accustomed to fight along with Switzers, it does not appear that they can now conquer without them. Hence it arises that the French cannot stand against the Switzers, and without the Switzers they do not come off well against others. The armies of the French have thus become mixed, partly mercenary and partly national, both of which arms together are much better than mercenaries alone or auxiliaries alone, yet much inferior to one's own forces. And this example proves it, the kingdom of France would be unconquerable if the ordinance of Charles had been enlarged or maintained.

But the scanty wisdom of man, on entering into an affair which looks well at first, cannot discern the poison that is hidden in it, as I have said above of consumption. Therefore, if he who rules a principality cannot recognize evils until they are upon him, he is not truly wise; and this insight is given to few.

And if the first disaster to the Roman Empire should be examined, it will be found to have commenced only with the enlisting of the Goths; because from that time the vigour of the Roman Empire began to decline, and all that valour which had raised it passed away to others.

I conclude, therefore, that no principality is secure without having its own forces; on the contrary, it is entirely dependent on good fortune, not having the valour which in adversity would defend it. And it has always been the opinion and judgment of wise men that nothing can be so uncertain or unstable as fame or power not founded on its own strength. And one's own forces are those which are composed either of subjects, citizens, or dependants; all others are mercenaries or auxiliaries. And the way to make ready one's own forces will be easily found if the rules suggested by me shall be reflected upon, and if one will consider how Philip, the father of Alexander the Great, and many republics and princes have armed and organized themselves, to which rules I entirely commit myself.

CHAPTER XIV

THAT WHICH CONCERNS A PRINCE
ON THE SUBJECT OF THE ART OF WAR

A PRINCE ought to have no other aim or thought, nor select anything else for his study, than war and its rules and discipline; for this is the sole art that belongs to him who rules, and it is of such force that it not only upholds those who are born princes, but it often enables men to rise from a private station to that rank. And, on the contrary, it is seen that when princes have thought more of ease than of arms they have lost their states. And the first cause of your losing it is to neglect this art; and what enables you to acquire a state is to be master of the art. Francesco Sforza, through being martial, from a private person became duke of Milan; and the sons, through avoiding the hardships and troubles of arms, from dukes became private persons. For among other evils which being unarmed brings you, it causes you to be despised, and this is one of those ignominies against which a prince ought to guard himself, as is shown later on. Because there is nothing proportionate between the armed and the unarmed; and it is not reasonable that he who is armed should yield obedience willingly to him who is unarmed, or that the unarmed man should be secure among armed servants. Because, there being in the one disdain and in the other suspicion, it is not possible for them to work well together. And therefore a prince who does not understand the art of war, over and above the other misfortunes already mentioned, cannot be respected by his soldiers, nor can he rely on them. He ought never, therefore, to have out of his thoughts this subject of war, and in peace he should addict himself more to its

Julius Caesar, who adorns this Umbrian plate, provided Renaissance Italians with a leading example of a great man from history.

exercise than in war; this he can do in two ways, the one by action, the other by study.

As regards action, he ought above all things to keep his men well organized and drilled, to follow incessantly the chase, by which he accustoms his body to hardships, and learns something of the nature of localities, and gets to find out how the mountains rise, how the valleys open out, how the plains lie, and to understand the nature of rivers and marshes, and in all this to take the greatest care. Which knowledge is useful in two ways. Firstly, he learns to know his country, and is better able to undertake its defence; afterwards, by means of the knowledge and observation of that locality, he understands with ease any other which it may be necessary for him to study hereafter; because the hills, valleys, and plains, and rivers and marshes that are, for instance, in Tuscany, have a certain resemblance to those of other countries, so that with a knowledge of the aspect of one country one can easily arrive at a knowledge of others. And the prince that lacks this skill lacks the essential which it is desirable that a captain should possess, for it teaches him to surprise his enemy, to select quarters, to lead armies, to array the battle, to besiege towns to advantage.

Philopoemen, prince of the Achaeans, among other praises which writers have bestowed on him, is commended because in time of peace he never had anything in his mind but the rules of war; and when he was in the country with friends, he often stopped and reasoned with them: "If the enemy should be upon that hill, and we should find ourselves here with our army, with whom would be the advantage? How should one best advance to meet him, keeping the ranks? If we should wish to retreat, how ought we to set about it? If they should retreat, how ought we to pursue?" And he would set forth to

them, as he went, all the chances that could befall an army; he would listen to their opinion and state his, confirming it with reasons, so that by these continual discussions there could never arise, in time of war, any unexpected circumstances that he could not deal with.

But to exercise the intellect the prince should read histories, and study there the actions of illustrious men, to see how they have borne themselves in war, to examine the causes of their victories and defeat, so as to avoid the latter and imitate the former; and above all do as an illustrious man did, who took as an exemplar one who had been praised and famous before him, and whose achievements and deeds he always kept in his mind, as it is said Alexander the Great imitated Achilles, Caesar Alexander, Scipio Cyrus. And whoever reads the life of Cyrus, written by Xenophon, will recognize afterwards in the life of Scipio how that imitation was his glory, and how in chastity, affability, humanity, and liberality Scipio conformed to those things which have been written of Cyrus by Xenophon. A wise prince ought to observe some such rules, and never in peaceful times stand idle, but increase his resources with industry in such a way that they may be available to him in adversity, so that if fortune changes it may find him prepared to resist her blows.

CHAPTER XV

CONCERNING THINGS FOR WHICH MEN, AND ESPECIALLY PRINCES, ARE PRAISED OR BLAMED

IT REMAINS now to see what ought to be the rules of conduct for a prince towards subjects and friends. And as I know that many have written on this point, I expect I shall be considered presumptuous in mentioning it again, especially as in discussing it I shall depart from the methods of other people. But, it being my intention to write a thing which shall be useful to him who apprehends it, it appears to me more appropriate to follow up the real truth of a matter than the imagination of it; for many have pictured republics and principalities which in fact have never been known or seen, because how one lives is so far distant from how one ought to live, that he who neglects what is done for what ought to be done, sooner effects his ruin than his preservation; for a man who wishes to act entirely up to his professions of virtue soon meets with what destroys him among so much that is evil.

Hence it is necessary for a prince wishing to hold his own to know how to do wrong, and to make use of it or not according to necessity. Therefore, putting on one side imaginary things concerning a prince, and discussing those which are real, I say that all men when they are spoken of, and chiefly princes for being more highly placed, are remarkable for some of those qualities which bring them either blame or praise; and thus it is that one is reputed liberal, another miserly, using a Tuscan term (because an avaricious person in our language is still he who desires to possess by robbery, whilst we

Lorenzo de Medici welcoming the Arts and Sciences to the Florentine court; painting from the Palazzo Pitti.

call one miserly who deprives himself too much of the use of his own); one is reputed generous, one rapacious; one cruel, one compassionate; one faithless, another faithful; one effeminate and cowardly, another bold and brave; one affable, another haughty; one lascivious, another chaste; one sincere, another cunning; one hard, another easy; one grave, another frivolous; one religious, another unbelieving, and the like. And I know that every one will confess that it would be most praiseworthy in a prince to exhibit all the above qualities that are considered good; but because they can neither be entirely possessed nor observed, for human conditions do not permit it, it is necessary for him to be sufficiently prudent that he may know how to avoid the reproach of those vices which would lose him his state; and also to keep himself, if it be possible, from those which would not lose him it; but this not being possible, he may with less hesitation abandon himself to them. And again, he need not make himself uneasy at incurring a reproach for those vices without which the state can only be saved with difficulty, for if everything is considered carefully, it will be found that something which looks like virtue, if followed, would be his ruin; whilst something else, which looks like vice, yet followed, brings him security and prosperity.

Borso d'Este, first duke of Ferrara and patron of the arts, appears just and benevolent in a fresco commissioned for the Palazzo Schifanoia.

CHAPTER XVI

CONCERNING LIBERALITY AND MEANNESS

COMMENCING then with the first of the above-named characteristics, I say that it would be well to be reputed liberal. Nevertheless, liberality exercised in a way that does not bring you the reputation for it, injures you; for if one exercises it honestly and as it should be exercised, it may not become known, and you will not avoid the reproach of its opposite. Therefore, anyone wishing to maintain among men the name of liberal is obliged to avoid no attribute of magnificence; so that a prince thus inclined will consume in such acts all his property, and will be compelled in the end, if he wish to maintain the name of liberal, to unduly weigh down his people, and tax them, and do everything he can to get money. This will soon make him odious to his subjects, and becoming poor he will be little valued by anyone; thus, with his liberality, having offended many and rewarded few, he is affected by the very first trouble and imperilled by whatever may be the first danger; recognizing this himself, and wishing to draw back from it, he runs at once into the reproach of being miserly.

Therefore, a prince, not being able to exercise this virtue of liberality in such a way that it is recognized, except to his cost, if he is wise he ought not to fear the reputation of being mean, for in time he will come to be more considered than if liberal, seeing that with his economy his revenues are enough, that he can defend himself against all attacks, and is able to engage in enterprises without burdening his people; thus it comes to pass that he exercises liberality

---

Pope Julius II, by Raphael. At one time having a reputation for liberality, Giuliano Della Rovere is remembered as the "warrior pope".

towards all from whom he does not take, who are numberless, and meanness towards those to whom he does not give, who are few.

We have not seen great things done in our time except by those who have been considered mean; the rest have failed. Pope Julius II was assisted in reaching the papacy by a reputation for liberality, yet he did not strive afterwards to keep it up, when he made war on the king of France; and he made many wars without imposing any extraordinary tax on his subjects, for he supplied his additional expenses out of his long thriftiness. The present king of Spain would not have undertaken or conquered in so many enterprises if he had been reputed liberal. A prince, therefore, provided that he has not to rob his subjects, that he can defend himself, that he does not become poor and abject, that he is not forced to become rapacious, ought to hold of little account a reputation for being mean, for it is one of those vices which will enable him to govern.

And if anyone should say: Caesar obtained empire by liberality, and many others have reached the highest positions by having been liberal, and by being considered so, I answer: Either you are a prince in fact, or in a way to become one. In the first case this liberality is dangerous, in the second it is very necessary to be considered liberal; and Caesar was one of those who wished to become pre-eminent in Rome; but if he had survived after becoming so, and had not moderated his expenses, he would have destroyed his government. And if anyone should reply: Many have been princes, and have done great things with armies, who have been considered very liberal, I reply: Either a prince spends that which is his own or his subjects' or else that of others. In the first case he ought to be sparing, in the second he ought not to neglect any opportunity for liberality. And to the price who goes forth with his army,

supporting it by pillage, sack, and extortion, handling that which belongs to others, this liberality is necessary, otherwise he would not be followed by soldiers. And of that which is neither yours nor your subjects' you can be a ready giver, as were Cyrus, Caesar, and Alexander; because it does not take away your reputation if you squander that of others, but adds to it; it is only squandering your own that injures you.

And there is nothing wastes so rapidly as liberality, for even whilst you exercise it you lose the power to do so, and so become either poor or despised, or else, in avoiding poverty, rapacious and hated. And a prince should guard himself, above all things, against being despised and hated; and liberality leads you to both. Therefore it is wiser to have a reputation for meanness which brings reproach without hatred, than to be compelled through seeking a reputation for liberality to incur a name for rapacity which begets reproach with hatred.

CHAPTER XVII

CONCERNING CRUELTY AND CLEMENCY, AND WHETHER IT IS BETTER TO BE LOVED THAN FEARED

COMING now to the other qualities mentioned above, I say that every prince ought to desire to be considered clement and not cruel. Nevertheless he ought to take care not to misuse this clemency. Cesare Borgia was considered cruel; notwithstanding, his cruelty reconciled the Romagna, unified it, and restored it to peace and loyalty. And if this be rightly considered, he will be seen to have been much more merciful than the Florentine people, who, to avoid a reputation for cruelty, permitted Pistoia to be destroyed. Therefore a prince, so long as he keeps his subjects united and loyal, ought not to mind the reproach of cruelty; because with a few examples he will be more merciful than those who, through too much mercy, allow disorders to arise, from which follow murders or robberies; for these are wont to injure the whole people, whilst those executions which originate with a prince offend the individual only.

And of all princes, it is impossible for the new prince to avoid the imputation of cruelty, owing to new states being full of dangers. Hence Virgil, through the mouth of Dido, excuses the inhumanity of her reign owing to its being new, saying:

Res dura, et regni novitas me talia cogunt
Moliri, et late fines custode tueri.[1]

Pallas Chases the Vices from the Garden of Virtue *(1502, detail)*
by Mantegna; the fleeing ape represents immortal hatred.

Nevertheless he ought to be slow to believe and to act, nor should he himself show fear, but proceed in a temperate manner with prudence and humanity, so that too much confidence may not make him incautious and too much distrust render him intolerable.

Upon this a question arises: whether it be better to be loved than feared or feared than loved? It may be answered that one should wish to be both, but, because it is difficult to unite them in one person, is much safer to be feared than loved, when, of the two, either must be dispensed with. Because this is to be asserted in general of men, that they are ungrateful, fickle, false, cowardly, covetous, and as long as you succeed they are yours entirely; they will offer you their blood, property, life and children, as is said above, when the need is far distant; but when it approaches they turn against you. And that prince who, relying entirely on their promises, has neglected other precautions, is ruined; because friendships that are obtained by payments, and not by greatness or nobility of mind, may indeed be earned, but they are not secured, and in time of need cannot be relied upon; and men have less scruple in offending one who is beloved than one who is feared, for love is preserved by the link of obligation which, owing to the baseness of men, is broken at every opportunity for their advantage; but fear preserves you by a dread of punishment which never fails.

Nevertheless a prince ought to inspire fear in such a way that, if he does not win love, he avoids hatred; because he can endure very well being feared whilst he is not hated, which will always be as long as he abstains from the property of his citizens and subjects and from their women. But when it is necessary for him to proceed against the life of someone, he must do it on proper justification and for manifest cause, but above all things he must keep

his hands off the property of others, because men more quickly forget the death of their father than the loss of their patrimony. Besides, pretexts for taking away the property are never wanting; for he who has once begun to live by robbery will always find pretexts for seizing what belongs to others; but reasons for taking life, on the contrary, are more difficult to find and sooner lapse. But when a prince is with his army, and has under control a multitude of soldiers, then it is quite necessary for him to disregard the reputation of cruelty, for without it he would never hold his army united or disposed to its duties.

Among the wonderful deeds of Hannibal this one is enumerated: that having led an enormous army, composed of many various races of men, to fight in foreign lands, no dissensions arose either among them or against the prince, whether in his bad or in his good fortune. This arose from nothing else than his inhuman cruelty, which, with his boundless valour, made him revered and terrible in the sight of his soldiers, but without that cruelty, his other virtues were not sufficient to produce this effect. And shortsighted writers admire his deeds from one point of view and from another condemn the principal cause of them. That it is true his other virtues would not have been sufficient for him may be proved by the case of Scipio, that most excellent man, not of his own times but within the memory of man, against whom, nevertheless, his army rebelled in Spain; this arose from nothing but his too great forbearance, which gave his soldiers more licence than is consistent with military discipline. For this he was upbraided in the Senate by Fabius Maximus, and called the corrupter of the Roman soldiery. The Locrians were laid waste by a legate of Scipio, yet they were not avenged by him, nor was the insolence of the legate punished, owing entirely to his easy nature. Insomuch that someone in the Senate, wishing to excuse him, said there were many men who knew much better how not to err than to correct the errors of others. This

disposition, if he had been continued in the command, would have destroyed in time the fame and glory of Scipio; but, he being under the control of the Senate, this injurious characteristic not only concealed itself, but contributed to his glory.

Returning to the question of being feared or loved, I come to the conclusion that, men loving according to their own will and fearing according to that of the prince, a wise prince should establish himself on that which is in his own control and not in that of others; he must endeavour only to avoid hatred, as is noted.

NOTES FOR CHAPTER XVII
[1] *"...against my will, my fate,*
A throne unsettled, and an infant state,
Bid me defend my realms with all my pow'rs,
And guard with these severities my shores."

Hannibal In Italy, *one of four frescoes of the Punic Wars by Jacopo Ripanda in the Hannibal Hall, Museo Capitolino, Rome.*

THE ART OF POWER

CHAPTER XVIII

CONCERNING THE WAY IN WHICH PRINCES SHOULD KEEP FAITH

EVERY one admits how praiseworthy it is in a prince to keep faith, and to live with integrity and not with craft. Nevertheless our experience has been that those princes who have done great things have held good faith of little account, and have known how to circumvent the intellect of men by craft, and in the end have overcome those who have relied on their word. You must know there are two ways of contesting, the one by the law, the other by force; the first method is proper to men, the second to beasts; but because the first is frequently not sufficient, it is necessary to have recourse to the second. Therefore it is necessary for a prince to understand how to avail himself of the beast and the man. This has been figuratively taught to princes by ancient writers, who describe how Achilles and many other princes of old were given to the Centaur Chiron to nurse, who brought them up in his discipline; which means solely that, as they had for a teacher one who was half beast and half man, so it is necessary for a prince to know how to make use of both natures, and that one without the other is not durable. A prince, therefore, being compelled knowingly to adopt the beast, ought to choose the fox and the lion; because the lion cannot defend himself against snares and the fox cannot defend himself against wolves. Therefore, it is necessary to be a fox to discover the snares and a lion to terrify the wolves. Those who rely simply on the lion do not understand what they are about. Therefore a wise lord cannot, nor ought he to, keep faith when such observance may be turned against him, and when the reasons that caused him to pledge it exist no longer. If

---

*Minerva and the Centaur by Botticelli (detail) symbolizes the dual
nature of the human soul, with reason triumphant over instinct.*

men were entirely good this precept would not hold, but because they are bad, and will not keep faith with you, you too are not bound to observe it with them. Nor will there ever be wanting to a prince legitimate reasons to excuse this nonobservance. Of this endless modern examples could be given, showing how many treaties and engagements have been made void and of no effect through the faithlessness of princes; and he who has known best how to employ the fox has succeeded best.

But it is necessary to know well how to disguise this characteristic, and to be a great pretender and dissembler; and men are so simple, and so subject to present necessities, that he who seeks to deceive will always find someone who will allow himself to be deceived. One recent example I cannot pass over in silence. Alexander VI did nothing else but deceive men, nor ever thought of doing otherwise, and he always found victims; for there never was a man who had greater power in asserting, or who with greater oaths would affirm a thing, yet would observe it less; nevertheless his deceits always succeeded according to his wishes, because he well understood this side of mankind.

Therefore it is unnecessary for a prince to have all the good qualities I have enumerated, but it is very necessary to appear to have them. And I shall dare to say this also, that to have them and always to observe them is injurious, and that to appear to have them is useful; to appear merciful, faithful, humane, religious, upright, and to be so, but with a mind so framed that should you require not to be so, you may be able and know how to change to the opposite.

A Leonardo da Vinci drawing of a lion, one of two beasts — with the fox — whose nature Machiavelli argued was worth imitation by princes.

And you have to understand this, that a prince, especially a new one, cannot observe all those things for which men are esteemed, being often forced, in order to maintain the state, to act contrary to faith, friendship, humanity, and religion. Therefore it is necessary for him to have a mind ready to turn itself accordingly as the winds and variations of fortune force it, yet, as I have said above, not to diverge from the good if he can avoid doing so, but, if compelled, then to know how to set about it.

For this reason a prince ought to take care that he never lets anything slip from his lips that is not replete with the above-named five qualities, that he

may appear to him who sees and hears him altogether merciful, faithful, humane, upright, and religious. There is nothing more necessary to appear to have than this last quality, inasmuch as men judge generally more by the eye than by the hand, because it belongs to everybody to see you, to few to come in touch with you. Everyone sees what you appear to be, few really know what you are, and those few dare not oppose themselves to the opinion of the many, who have the majesty of the state to defend them; and in the actions of all men, and especially of princes, which it is not prudent to challenge, one judges by the result.

For that reason, let a prince have the credit of conquering and holding his state, the means will always be considered honest, and he will be praised by everybody because the vulgar are always taken by what a thing seems to be and by what comes of it; and in the world there are only the vulgar, for the few find a place there only when the many have no ground to rest on.

One prince[1] of the present time, whom it is not well to name, never preaches anything else but peace and good faith, and to both he is most hostile, and either, if he had kept it, would have deprived him of reputation and kingdom many a time.

NOTES FOR CHAPTER XVIII

[1] *Ferdinand of Aragon, who disputed control of Italy with various kings of France, allying himself with Maximilian I, Holy Roman Emperor, to expel the French from Naples.*

Maximilian I and his family. To consolidate his realm the Habsburg emperor made telling use of strategic marriages for his children.

MAXIMILIANVS I IMP.
ARCHIDVX AVSTRIÆ.
DVX BVRGVNDIÆ.

PHILIPPVS HISP. REX. I.
ARCHIDVX AVSTRIÆ.

MARIA DVCISSA
BVRGVNDIÆ MAX: VXOR.

FERDINANDVS. I. IMP.
ARCHIDVX AVSTRIÆ.

CAROLVS. V. IMP.
ARCHIDVX. AVSTRIÆ.

LVDOVICVS REX
HVNG MAS.

CHAPTER XIX

THAT ONE SHOULD AVOID BEING DESPISED AND HATED

NOW, concerning the characteristics of which mention is made above, I have spoken of the more important ones, the others I wish to discuss briefly under this generality, that the prince must consider, as has been in part said before, how to avoid those things which will make him hated or contemptible; and as often as he shall have succeeded he will have fulfilled his part, and he need not fear any danger in other reproaches.

It makes him hated above all things, as I have said, to be rapacious, and to be a violator of the property and women of his subjects, from both of which he must abstain. And when neither their property nor honour is touched, the majority of men live content, and he has only to contend with the ambition of a few, whom he can curb with ease in many ways.

It makes him contemptible to be considered fickle, frivolous, effeminate, mean-spirited, irresolute, from all of which a prince should guard himself as from a rock; and he should endeavour to show in his actions greatness, courage, gravity, and fortitude; and in his private dealings with his subjects let him show that his judgments are irrevocable, and maintain himself in such reputation that no one can hope either to deceive him or to get round him.

Marcus Aurelius, brought up to prize manliness without ostentation and respected as honest and just, is petitioned by defeated leaders.

That prince is highly esteemed who conveys this impression of himself, and he who is highly esteemed is not easily conspired against; for, provided it is well known that he is an excellent man and revered by his people, he can only be attacked with difficulty. For this reason a prince ought to have two fears, one from within, on account of his subjects, the other from without, on account of external powers. From the latter he is defended by being well armed and having good allies, and if he is well armed he will have good friends, and affairs will always remain quiet within when they are quiet without, unless they should have been already disturbed by conspiracy; and even should affairs outside be disturbed, if he has carried out his preparations and has lived as I have said, as long as he does not despair, he will resist every attack, as I said Nabis the Spartan did.

But concerning his subjects, when affairs outside are disturbed he has only to fear that they will conspire secretly, from which a prince can easily secure himself by avoiding being hated and despised, and by keeping the people satisfied with him, which it is most necessary for him to accomplish, as I said above at length. And one of the most efficacious remedies that a prince can have against conspiracies is not to be hated and despised by the people, for he who conspires against a prince always expects to please them by his removal; but when the conspirator can only look forward to offending them, he will not have the courage to take such a course, for the difficulties that confront a conspirator are infinite. And as experience shows, many have been the conspiracies, but few have been successful; because he who conspires cannot act alone, nor can he take a companion except from those whom he believes to be malcontents, and as soon as you have opened your mind to a malcontent you have given him the material with which to content himself, for by denouncing you he can look for every advantage; so that, seeing the gain from this course to be assured, and seeing the other to be doubtful and full of dangers, he must be a very rare friend, or a thoroughly obstinate enemy of the prince, to keep faith with you.

And, to reduce the matter into a small compass, I say that, on the side of the conspirator, there is nothing but fear, jealousy, prospect of punishment to terrify him; but on the side of the prince there is the majesty of the principality, the laws, the protection of friends and the state to defend him; so that, adding to all these things the popular goodwill, it is impossible that any one should be so rash as to conspire. For whereas in general the conspirator has to fear before the execution of his plot, in this case he has also to fear the sequel to the crime; because on account of it he has the people for an enemy, and thus cannot hope for any escape.

Endless examples could be given on this subject, but I will be content with one, brought to pass within the memory of our fathers. Messer Annibale Bentivoglio, who was prince in Bologna (grandfather of the present Annibale), having been murdered by the Canneschi, who had conspired against him, not one of his family survived but Messer Giovanni, who was in childhood: immediately after his assassination the people rose and murdered all the Canneschi. This sprung from the popular goodwill which the house of Bentivoglio enjoyed in those days in Bologna; which was so great that, although none remained there after the death of Annibale who were able to rule the state, the Bolognese, having information that there was one of the Bentivoglio family in Florence, who up to that time had been considered the son of a blacksmith, sent to Florence for him and gave him the government of their city, and it was ruled by him until Messer Giovanni came in due course to the government.

For this reason I consider that a prince ought to reckon conspiracies of little account when his people hold him in esteem; but when it is hostile to him, and bears hatred towards him, he ought to fear everything and everybody. And well-ordered states and wise princes have taken every care not to drive

the nobles to desperation, and to keep the people satisfied and contented, for this is one of the most important objects a prince can have.

Among the best ordered and governed kingdoms of our times is France, and in it are found many good institutions on which depend the liberty and security of the king; of these the first is the parliament and its authority, because he who founded the kingdom, knowing the ambition of the nobility and their boldness, considered that a bit in their mouths would be necessary to hold them in; and, on the other side, knowing the hatred of the people, founded in fear, against the nobles, he wished to protect them, yet he was not anxious for this to be the particular care of the king; therefore, to take away the reproach which he would be liable to from the nobles for favouring the people, and from the people for favouring the nobles, he set up an arbiter, who should be one who could beat down the great and favour the lesser without reproach to the king. Neither could you have a better or a more prudent arrangement, or a greater source of security to the king and kingdom. From this one can draw another important conclusion, that princes ought to leave affairs of reproach to the management of others, and keep those of grace in their own hands. And further, I consider that a prince ought to cherish the nobles, but not so as to make himself hated by the people.

It may appear, perhaps, to some who have examined the lives and deaths of the Roman emperors that many of them would be an example contrary to my opinion, seeing that some of them lived nobly and showed great qualities of soul, nevertheless they have lost their empire or have been killed by subjects who have conspired against them. Wishing, therefore, to answer these objections, I will recall the characters of some of the emperors, and will show that the causes of their ruin were not different to those alleged by me; at the same

time I will only submit for consideration those things that are noteworthy to him who studies the affairs of those times.

It seems to me sufficient to take all those emperors who succeeded to the empire from Marcus the philosopher down to Maximinus; they were Marcus and his son Commodus, Pertinax, Julian, Severus and his son Antoninus Caracalla, Macrinus, Heliogabalus, Alexander, and Maximinus.

There is first to note that, whereas in other principalities the ambition of the nobles and the insolence of the people only have to be contended with, the Roman emperors had a third difficulty in having to put up with the cruelty and avarice of their soldiers, a matter so beset with difficulties that it was the ruin of many; for it was a hard thing to give satisfaction both to soldiers and people; because the people loved peace, and for this reason they loved the unaspiring prince, whilst the soldiers loved the warlike prince who was bold, cruel, and rapacious, which qualities they were quite willing he should exercise upon the people, so that they could get double pay and give vent to their greed and cruelty. Hence it arose that those emperors were always overthrown who, either by birth or training, had no great authority, and most of them, especially those who came new to the principality, recognizing the difficulty of these two opposing humours, were inclined to give satisfaction to the soldiers, caring little about injuring the people. Which course was necessary, because, as princes cannot help being hated by someone, they ought, in the first place, to avoid being hated by everyone, and when they cannot compass this, they ought to endeavour with the utmost diligence to avoid the hatred of the most powerful. Therefore, those emperors who through inexperience had need of special favour adhered more readily to the soldiers than to the people; a course which turned out advantageous

to them or not, accordingly as the prince knew how to maintain authority over them.

From these causes it arose that Marcus [Aurelius], Pertinax, and Alexander, being all men of modest life, lovers of justice, enemies to cruelty, humane, and benignant, came to a sad end except Marcus; he alone lived and died honoured, because he had succeeded to the throne by hereditary title, and owed nothing either to the soldiers or the people; and afterwards, being possessed of many virtues which made him respected, he always kept both orders in their places whilst he lived, and was neither hated nor despised.

But Pertinax was created emperor against the wishes of the soldiers, who, being accustomed to live licentiously under Commodus, could not endure the honest life to which Pertinax wished to reduce them; thus, having given cause for hatred, to which hatred there was added contempt for his old age, he was overthrown at the very beginning of his administration. And here it should be noted that hatred is acquired as much by good works as by bad ones, therefore, as I said before, a prince wishing to keep his state is very often forced to do evil; for when that body is corrupt whom you think you have need of to maintain yourself – it may be either the people or the soldiers or the nobles – you have to submit to its humours and to gratify them, and then good works will do you harm.

But let us come to Alexander, who was a man of such great goodness, that

Violante Bentivoglio (left, detail), depicted as a donor of an altarpiece. Her family was powerful in Bologna until exiled by rivals.

among the other praises which are accorded him is this, that in the fourteen years he held the empire no one was ever put to death by him unjudged; nevertheless, being considered effeminate and a man who allowed himself to be governed by his mother, he became despised, the army conspired against him, and murdered him.

Turning now to the opposite characters of Commodus, Severus, Antoninus Caracalla, and Maximinus, you will find them all cruel and rapacious – men who, to satisfy their soldiers, did not hesitate to commit every kind of iniquity against the people; and all, except Severus, came to a bad end; but in Severus there was so much valour that, keeping the soldiers friendly, although the people were oppressed by him, he reigned successfully; for his valour made him so much admired in the sight of the soldiers and people that the latter were kept in a way astonished and awed and the former respectful and satisfied. And because the actions of this man, as a new prince, were great, I wish to show briefly that he knew well how to counterfeit the fox and the lion, which natures, as I said above, it is necessary for a prince to imitate.

Knowing the sloth of the Emperor Julian, he persuaded the army in Sclavonia, of which he was captain, that it would be right to go to Rome and avenge the death of Pertinax, who had been killed by the praetorian soldiers; and under this pretext, without appearing to aspire to the throne, he moved the army on Rome, and reached Italy before it was known that he had started. On his arrival at Rome, the Senate, through fear, elected him emperor and killed Julian. After this there remained for Severus, who wished to make himself master of the whole empire, two difficulties; one in Asia, where Niger, head of the Asiatic army, had caused himself to be proclaimed emperor; the other in the west where Albinus was, who also aspired to the throne. And

as he considered it dangerous to declare himself hostile to both, he decided to attack Niger and to deceive Albinus. To the latter he wrote that, being elected emperor by the Senate, he was willing to share that dignity with him and sent him the title of Caesar; and, moreover, that the Senate had made Albinus his colleague; which things were accepted by Albinus as true. But after Severus had conquered and killed Niger, and settled oriental affairs, he returned to Rome and complained to the Senate that Albinus, little recognizing the benefits that he had received from him, had by treachery sought to murder him, and for this ingratitude he was compelled to punish him. Afterwards he sought him out in France, and took from him his government and life. He who will, therefore, carefully examine the actions of this man will find him a most valiant lion and a most cunning fox; he will find him feared and respected by everyone, and not hated by the army; and it need not be wondered at that he, a new man, was able to hold the empire so well, because his supreme renown always protected him from that hatred which the people might have conceived against him for his violence.

But his son Antoninus was a most eminent man, and had very excellent qualities, which made him admirable in the sight of the people and acceptable to the soldiers, for he was a warlike man, most enduring of fatigue, a despiser of all delicate food and other luxuries, which caused him to be beloved by the armies. Nevertheless, his ferocity and cruelties were so great and so unheard of that, after endless single murders, he killed a large number of the people of Rome and all those of Alexandria. He became hated by the whole world, and also feared by those he had around him, to such an extent that he was murdered in the midst of his army by a centurion. And here it must be noted that such-like deaths, which are deliberately inflicted with a resolved and desperate courage, cannot be avoided by princes, because anyone who does not fear to die can inflict them; but a prince may fear them the less because they are

very rare; he has only to be careful not to do any grave injury to those whom he employs or has around him in the service of the state. Antoninus had not taken this care, but had contumeliously killed a brother of that centurion, whom also he daily threatened, yet retained in his bodyguard; which, as it turned out, was a rash thing to do, and proved the emperor's ruin.

But let us come to Commodus, to whom it should have been very easy to hold the empire, for, being the son of Marcus, he had inherited it, and he had only to follow in the footsteps of his father to please his people and soldiers; but, being by nature cruel and brutal, he gave himself up to amusing the soldiers and corrupting them, so that he might indulge his rapacity upon the people; on the other hand, not maintaining his dignity, often descending to the theatre to compete with gladiators, and doing other vile things, little worthy of the imperial majesty, he fell into contempt with the soldiers, and being hated by one party and despised by the other, he was conspired against and killed.

It remains to discuss the character of Maximinus. He was a very warlike man, and the armies, being disgusted with the effeminacy of Alexander, of whom I have already spoken, killed him and elected Maximinus to the throne. This he did not possess for long, for two things made him hated and despised; the one, his having kept sheep in Thrace, which brought him into contempt (it being well known to all, and considered a great indignity by everyone), and the other, his having at the accession to his dominions deferred going to Rome and taking possession of the imperial seat; he had also gained a reputation for the utmost ferocity by having, through his prefects in Rome and elsewhere in the empire, practised many cruelties, so that the whole world was moved to anger at the meanness of his birth and to fear at his barbarity.

First Africa rebelled, then the Senate with all the people of Rome, and all Italy conspired against him, to which may be added his own army: this latter, besieging Aquileia and meeting with difficulties in taking it, were disgusted with his cruelties, and fearing him less when they found so many against him, murdered him.

I do not wish to discuss Heliogabalus, Macrinus, or Julian, who, being thoroughly contemptible, were quickly wiped out; but I will bring this discourse to a conclusion by saying that princes in our times have this difficulty of giving inordinate satisfaction to their soldiers in a far less degree, because, notwithstanding one has to give them some indulgence, that is soon done; none of these princes have armies that are veterans in the governance and administration of provinces, as were the armies of the Roman Empire; and whereas it was then more necessary to give satisfaction to the soldiers than to the people, it is now more necessary to all princes, except the Turk and the Soldan, to satisfy the people rather than the soldiers, because the people are the more powerful.

From the above I have excepted the Turk, who always keeps round him twelve infantry and fifteen thousand cavalry on which depend the security and strength of the kingdom, and it is necessary that, putting aside every consideration for the people, he should keep them his friends. The kingdom of the Soldan is similar; being entirely in the hands of soldiers, it follows again that, without regard to the people, he must keep them his friends. But you must note that the state of the Soldan is unlike all other principalities, for the reason that it is like the Christian pontificate, which cannot be called either an hereditary or a newly formed principality; because the sons of the old prince not the heirs, but he who is elected to that position by those who

have authority, and the sons remain only noblemen. And this being an ancient custom, it cannot be called a new principality, because there are none of those difficulties in it that are met with in new ones; for although the prince is new, the constitution of the state is old, and it is framed so as to receive him as if he were its hereditary lord.

But returning to the subject of our discourse, I say that whoever will consider it will acknowledge that either hatred or contempt has been fatal to the above-named emperors, and it will be recognized also how it happened that, a number of them acting in one way and a number in another, only one in each

way came to a happy end and the rest to unhappy ones. Because it would have been useless and dangerous for Pertinax and Alexander, being new princes, to imitate Marcus, who was heir to the principality; and likewise it would have been utterly destructive to Caracalla, Commodus, and Maximinus to have imitated Severus, they not having sufficient valour to enable them to tread in his footsteps. Therefore a prince, new to the principality, cannot imitate the actions of Marcus, nor, again, is it necessary to follow those of Severus, but he ought to take from Severus those parts which are necessary to found his state, and from Marcus those which are proper and glorious to keep a state that may already be stable and firm.

C H A P T E R   X X

ARE FORTRESSES, AND MANY OTHER THINGS TO WHICH PRINCES
OFTEN RESORT, ADVANTAGEOUS OR HURTFUL?

SOME princes, so as to hold securely the state, have disarmed their subjects; others have kept their subject towns by factions; others have fostered enmities against themselves; others have laid themselves out to gain over those whom they distrusted in the beginning of their governments; some have built fortresses; some have overthrown and destroyed them. And although one cannot give a final judgment on all of these things unless one possesses the particulars of those states in which a decision has to be made, nevertheless I will speak as comprehensively as the matter of itself will admit.

There never was a new prince who has disarmed his subjects; rather when he has found them disarmed he has always armed them, because, by arming them, those arms become yours, those men who were distrusted become faithful, and those who were faithful are kept so, and your subjects become your adherents. And whereas all subjects cannot be armed, yet when those whom you do arm are benefited, the others can be handled more freely, and this difference in their treatment, which they quite understand, makes the former your dependents, and the latter, considering it to be necessary that those who have the most danger and service should have the most reward, excuse you. But when you disarm them, you at once offend them by showing that you distrust them, either for cowardice or for want of loyalty, and either of these opinions breeds hatred against you. And because you cannot remain

Between the towers of the Castelnuovo in Naples is the Alfonso I
Triumph Arch, built to commemmorate the king's arrival in 1443.

unarmed, it follows that you turn to mercenaries, which are of the character already shown; even if they should be good they would not be sufficient to defend you against powerful enemies and distrusted subjects. Therefore, as I have said, a new prince in a new principality has always distributed arms. Histories are full of examples. But when a prince acquires a new state, which he adds as a province to his old one, then it is necessary to disarm the men of that state, except those who have been his adherents in acquiring it; and these again, with time and opportunity, should be rendered soft and effeminate; and matters should be managed in such a way that all the armed men in the state shall be your own soldiers who in your old state were living near you.

Our forefathers, and those who were reckoned wise, were accustomed to say that it was necessary to hold Pistoia by factions and Pisa by fortresses; and with this idea they fostered quarrels in some of their tributary towns so as to keep possession of them the more easily. This may have been well enough in those times when Italy was in a way balanced, but I do not believe that it can be accepted as a precept for today, because I do not believe that factions can ever be of use; rather it is certain that when the enemy comes upon you in divided cities you are quickly lost, because the weakest party will always assist the outside forces and the other will not be able to resist. The Venetians, moved, as I believe, by the above reasons, fostered the Guelph and Ghibelline factions in their tributary cities; and although they never allowed them to come to bloodshed, yet they nursed these disputes amongst them, so that the citizens, distracted by their differences, should not unite against them. Which, as we saw, did not afterwards turn out as expected, because, after the rout at Vaila, one party at once took courage and seized the state. Such methods argue, therefore, weakness in the prince, because these factions will never be permitted in a vigorous principality; such methods for enabling one

the more easily to manage subjects are only useful in times of peace, but if war comes this policy proves fallacious.

Without doubt princes become great when they overcome the difficulties and obstacles by which they are confronted, and therefore fortune, especially when she desires to make a great new prince, who has a greater necessity to earn renown than an hereditary one, causes enemies to arise and form designs against him, in order that he may have the opportunity of overcoming them, and by them to mount higher, as by a ladder which his enemies have raised. For this reason many consider that a wise prince, when he has the opportunity, ought with craft to foster some animosity against himself, so that, having crushed it, his renown may rise higher.

Princes, especially new ones, have found more fidelity and assistance in those men who in the beginning of their rule were distrusted than among those who in the beginning were trusted. Pandolfo Petrucci, prince of Siena, ruled his state more by those who had been distrusted than by others. But on this question one cannot speak generally, for it varies so much with the individual; I will only say this, that those men who at the commencement of a princedom have been hostile, if they are of a description to need assistance to support themselves, can always be gained over with the greatest ease, and they will be tightly held to serve the prince with fidelity, inasmuch as they know it to be very necessary for them to cancel by deeds the bad impression which he had formed of them; and thus the prince always extracts more profit from them than from those who, serving him in too much security, may neglect his affairs. And since the matter demands it, I must not fail to warn a prince, who by means of secret favours has acquired a new state, that he must well consider the reasons which induced those to favour him who did

so; and if it be not a natural affection towards him, but only discontent with their government, then he will only keep them friendly with great trouble and difficulty, for it will be impossible to satisfy them. And weighing well the reasons for this in those examples which can be taken from ancient and modern affairs, we shall find that it is easier for the prince to make friends of those men who were contented under the former government, and are therefore his enemies, than of those who, being discontented with it, were favourable to him and encouraged him to seize it.

It has been a custom with princes, in order to hold their states more securely, to build fortresses that may serve as a bridle and bit to those who might design to work against them, and as a place of refuge from a first attack. I praise this system because it has been made use of formerly. Notwithstanding that, Messer Nicolo Vitelli in our times has been seen to demolish two fortresses in Citta di Castello so that he might keep that state; Guidubaldo, duke of Urbino, on returning to his dominion, whence he had been driven by Cesare Borgia, razed to the foundations all the fortresses in that province, and considered that without them it would be more difficult to lose it; the Bentivoglio returning to Bologna came to a similar decision. Fortresses, therefore, are useful or not according to circumstances; if they do you good in one way they injure you in another. And this question can be reasoned thus: the prince who has more to fear from the people than from foreigners ought to build fortresses, but he who has more to fear from foreigners than from the people ought to leave them alone. The castle of Milan, built by Francesco Sforza, has made, and will make, more trouble for the house of Sforza than any other disorder in the state. For this reason the best possible

Portrait of Federico da Montefeltro, duke of Urbino, and his son Guidobaldo, by Berruguete, ca. 1480 (detail).

fortress is — not to be hated by the people, because, although you may hold the fortresses, yet they will not save you if the people hate you, for there will never be wanting foreigners to assist a people who have taken arms against you. It has not been seen in our times that such fortresses have been of use to any prince, unless to the countess of Forli, when the count Girolamo, her consort, was killed; for by that means she was able to withstand the popular attack and wait for assistance from Milan, and thus recover her state; and the posture of affairs was such at that time that the foreigners could not assist the people. But fortresses were of little value to her afterwards when Cesare Borgia attacked her, and when the people, her enemy, were allied with foreigners. Therefore it would have been safer for her, both then and before, not to have been hated by the people than to have had the fortresses. All these things considered then, I shall praise him who builds fortresses as well as him who does not, and I shall blame whoever, trusting in them, cares little about being hated by the people.

This constellation illumination was commissioned in 1469 by Antonello Petrucci, a member of that powerful Sienese family.

CHAPTER XX

CHAPTER XXI

HOW A PRINCE SHOULD CONDUCT HIMSELF
SO AS TO GAIN RENOWN

NOTHING makes a prince so much esteemed as great enterprises and set-ting a fine example. We have in our time Ferdinand of Aragon, the present king of Spain. He can almost be called a new prince, because he has risen, by fame and glory, from being an insignificant king to be the foremost king in Christendom; and if you will consider his deeds you will find them all great and some of them extraordinary. In the beginning of his reign he attacked Granada, and this enterprise was the foundation of his dominions. He did this quietly at first and without any fear of hindrance, for he held the minds of the barons of Castile occupied in thinking of the war and not anticipat-ing any innovations; thus they did not perceive that by these means he was acquiring power and authority over them. He was able with the money of the Church and of the people to sustain his armies, and by that long war to lay the foundation for the military skill which has since distinguished him. Fur-ther, always using religion as a plea, so as to undertake greater schemes, he devoted himself with a pious cruelty to driving out and clearing his kingdom of the Moors; nor could there be a more admirable example, nor one more rare. Under this same cloak he assailed Africa, he came down on Italy, he has finally attacked France; and thus his achievements and designs have always been great, and have kept the minds of his people in suspense and admira-tion and occupied with the issue of them. And his actions have arisen in such a way, one out of the other, that men have never been given time to work steadily against him.

King Ferdinand II of Aragón and Queen Isabella of Castile. After reconquering Spain, the monarchs established a New World empire.

Again, it much assists a prince to set unusual examples in internal affairs, similar to those which are related of Messer Bernabo da Milano, who, when he had the opportunity, by anyone in civil life doing some extraordinary thing, either good or bad, would take some method of rewarding or punishing him, which would be much spoken about. And a prince ought, above all things, always to endeavour in every action to gain for himself the reputation of being a great and remarkable man.

A prince is also respected when he is either a true friend or a downright enemy, that to say, when, without any reservation, he declares himself in favour of one party against the other; which course will always be more advantageous than standing neutral; because if two of your powerful neighbours come to blows, they are of such a character that, if one of them conquers, you have either to fear him or not. In either case it will always be more advantageous for you to declare yourself and to make war strenuously; because, in the first case, if you do not declare yourself, you will invariably fall a prey to the conqueror, to the pleasure and satisfaction of him who has been conquered, and you will have no reasons to offer, nor anything to protect or to shelter you. Because he who conquers does not want doubtful friends who will not aid him in the time of trial; and he who loses will not harbour you because you did not willingly, sword in hand, court his fate.

Antiochus went into Greece, being sent for by the Aetolians to drive out the Romans. He sent envoys to the Achaeans, who were friends of the Romans, exhorting them to remain neutral; and on the other hand the Romans urged them to take up arms. This question came to be discussed in the council of the Achaeans, where the legate of Antiochus urged them to stand neutral. To this the Roman legate answered: "As for that which has been said, that it is better

and more advantageous for your state not to interfere in our war, nothing can be more erroneous; because by not interfering you will be left, without favour or consideration, the spoil of the conqueror." Thus it will always happen that he who is not your friend will demand your neutrality, whilst he who is your friend will entreat you to declare yourself with arms. And irresolute princes, to avoid present dangers, generally follow the neutral path, and are generally ruined. But when a prince declares himself gallantly in favour of one side, if the party with whom he allies himself conquers, although the victor may be powerful and may have him at his mercy, yet he is indebted to him, and there is established a bond of amity; and men are never so shameless as to become a monument of ingratitude by oppressing you. Victories after all are never so complete that the victor must not show some regard, especially to justice. But if he with whom you ally yourself loses, you may be sheltered by him, and whilst he is able he may aid you, and you become companions in a fortune that may rise again.

In the second case, when those who fight are of such a character that you have no anxiety as to who may conquer, so much the more is it greater prudence to be allied, because you assist at the destruction of one by the aid of another who, if he had been wise, would have saved him; and conquering, as it is impossible that he should not with your assistance, he remains at your discretion. And here it is to be noted that a prince ought to take care never to make an alliance with one more powerful than himself for the purpose of attacking others, unless necessity compels him, as is said above; because if he conquers you are at his discretion, and princes ought to avoid as much as possible being at the discretion of anyone. The Venetians joined with France against the duke of Milan, and this alliance, which caused their ruin, could have been avoided. But when it cannot be avoided, as happened to the Florentines when the pope and Spain sent armies to attack Lombardy, then in such a case, for the above reasons, the prince ought to favour one of the parties.

Never let any government imagine that it can choose perfectly safe courses; rather let it expect to have to take very doubtful ones, because it is found in ordinary affairs that one never seeks to avoid one trouble without running into another; but prudence consists in knowing how to distinguish the character of troubles, and for choice to take the lesser evil.

A prince ought also to show himself a patron of ability, and to honour the proficient in every art. At the same time he should encourage his citizens to practise their callings peaceably, both in commerce and agriculture, and in every other following, so that one should not be deterred from improving his possessions for fear lest they be taken away from him or another from opening up trade for fear of taxes; but the prince ought to offer rewards to whoever wishes to do these things and designs in any way to honour his city or state.

Further, he ought to entertain the people with festivals and spectacles at convenient seasons of the year; and as every city is divided into guilds or into societies, he ought to hold such bodies in esteem, and associate with them sometimes, and show himself an example of courtesy and liberality; nevertheless, always maintaining the majesty of his rank, for this he must never consent to abate in anything.

The Victory of the Venetians over Ferrarans at the Battle of
Polesella, *1509, by Bassano (detail)*.

THE ART OF POWER

CHAPTER XXII

CONCERNING THE SECRETARIES OF PRINCES

THE choice of servants is of no little importance to a prince, and they are good or not according to the discrimination of the prince. And the first opinion which one forms of a prince, and of his understanding, is by observing the men he has around him; and when they are capable and faithful he may always be considered wise, because he has known how to recognize the capable and to keep them faithful. But when they are otherwise one cannot form a good opinion of him, for the prime error which he made was in choosing them.

There were none who knew Messer Antonio da Venafro as the servant of Pandolfo Petrucci, prince of Siena, who would not consider Pandolfo to be a very clever man in having Venafro for his servant. Because there are three classes of intellects: one which comprehends by itself; another which appreciates what others comprehend; and a third which neither comprehends by itself nor by the showing of others; the first is the most excellent, the second is good, the third is useless. Therefore, it follows necessarily that, if Pandolfo was not in the first rank, he was in the second, for whenever one has judgment to know good or bad when it is said and done, although he himself may not have the initiative, yet he can recognize the good and the bad in his servant, and the one he can praise and the other correct; thus the servant cannot hope to deceive him, and is kept honest. But to enable a prince to form an opinion of his servant there is one test which never falls; when you see the servant thinking more of his own interests than of yours, and seeking inwardly his

Ludovico III Gonzaga, duke of Mantua, talking to his secretary Marsilio Andreasi, a fresco by Mantegna for the Palazzo Ducale.

own profit in everything, such a man will never make a good servant, nor will you ever be able to trust him; because he who has the state of another in his hands ought never to think of himself, but always of his prince, and never pay any attention to matters in which the prince is not concerned.

On the other hand, to keep his servant honest the prince ought to study him, honouring him, enriching him, doing him kindnesses, sharing with him the honours and cares; and at the same time let him see that he cannot stand alone, so that many honours not make him desire more, many riches make him wish for more, and that many cares may make him dread changes. When, therefore, servants, and princes towards servants, are thus disposed, they can trust each other, but when it is otherwise, the end will always be disastrous for either one or the other.

People of the Court of the Sforza family *(detail), by Bonifacio Bembo. Under Sforza rule for more than a century, Milan flourished.*

CHAPTER XXIII

HOW FLATTERERS SHOULD BE AVOIDED

I DO NOT wish to leave out an important branch of this subject, for it is a danger from which princes are with difficulty preserved, unless they are very careful and discriminating. It is that of flatterers, of whom courts are full, because men are so self-complacent in their own affairs, and in a way so deceived in them, that they are preserved with difficulty from this pest, and if they wish to defend themselves they run the danger of falling into contempt. Because there is no other way of guarding oneself from flatterers except letting men understand that to tell you the truth does not offend you; but when everyone may tell you the truth, respect for you abates.

Therefore a wise prince ought to hold a third course by choosing the wise men in his state, and giving to them only the liberty of speaking the truth to him, and then only of those things of which he inquires, and of none others; but he ought to question them upon everything, and listen to their opinions, and afterwards form his own conclusions. With these counsellors, separately and collectively, he ought to carry himself in such a way that each of them should know that, the more freely he shall speak, the more he shall be preferred; outside of these, he should listen to no one, pursue the thing resolved on, and be steadfast in his resolutions. He who does otherwise is either overthrown by flatterers, or is so often changed by varying opinions that he falls into contempt. I wish on this subject to adduce a modern example. Fra Luca, the man of affairs to Maximilian, the present emperor, speaking of his

Homage of the people to Lorenzo de Medici, *by Vasari. In 1486 the sultan of Egypt sent a giraffe as a gift, causing a stir in the city.*

majesty, said: He consulted with no one, yet never got his own way in anything. This arose because of his following a practice the opposite to the above; for the emperor is a secretive man – he does not communicate his designs to anyone, nor does he receive opinions on them. But as in carrying them into effect they become revealed and known, they are at once obstructed by those men whom he has around him, and he, being pliant, is diverted from them. Hence it follows that those things he does one day he undoes the next, and no one ever understands what he wishes or intends to do, and no one can rely on his resolutions.

A prince, therefore, ought always to take counsel, but only when he wishes and not when others wish; he ought rather to discourage everyone from offering advice unless he asks it; but, however, he ought to be a constant inquirer, and afterwards a patient listener concerning the things of which he inquired; also, on learning that anyone, on any consideration, has not told him the truth, he should let his anger be felt.

And if there are some who think that a prince who conveys an impression of his wisdom is not so through his own ability, but through the good advisers that he has around him, beyond doubt they are deceived, because this is an axiom which never fails: that a prince who is not wise himself will never take good advice, unless by chance he has yielded his affairs entirely to one person who happens to be a very prudent man. In this case indeed he may be well governed, but it would not be for long, because such a governor would in a short time take away his state from him.

But if a prince who is not experienced should take counsel from more than one he will never get united counsels, nor will he know how to unite them.

THE ART OF POWER

Each of the counsellors will think of his own interests, and the prince will not know how to control them or to see through them. And they are not to be found otherwise, because men will always prove untrue to you unless they are kept honest by constraint. Therefore it must be inferred that good counsels, whencesoever they come, are born of the wisdom of the prince, and not the wisdom of the prince from good counsels.

CHAPTER XXIV

WHY THE PRINCES OF ITALY HAVE LOST THEIR STATES

THE previous suggestions, carefully observed, will enable a new prince to appear well established, and render him at once more secure and fixed in the state than if he had been long seated there. For the actions of a new prince are more narrowly observed than those of an hereditary one, and when they are seen to be able they gain more men and bind far tighter than ancient blood; because men are attracted more by the present than by the past, and when they find the present good they enjoy it and seek no further; they will also make the utmost defence for a prince if he fails them not in other things. Thus it will be a double glory to him to have established a new principality, and adorned and strengthened it with good laws, good arms, good allies, and with a good example; so will it be a double disgrace to him who, born a prince, shall lose his state by want of wisdom.

And if those seigniors are considered who have lost their states in Italy in our times, such as the king of Naples, the duke of Milan, and others, there will be found in them, firstly, one common defect in regard to arms from the causes which have been discussed at length; in the next place, some one of them will be seen, either to have had the people hostile, or if he has had the people friendly, he has not known how to secure the nobles. In the absence of these defects states that have power enough to keep an army in the field cannot be lost.

Francesco Sforza, painted by Bembo. In 1447 the Visconti line died out and in 1450 Sforza became the new duke of Milan.

Philip of Macedon, not the father of Alexander the Great, but he who was conquered by Titus Quintius, had not much territory compared to the greatness of the Romans and the Greeks who attacked him, yet being a warlike man who knew how to attract the people and secure the nobles, he sustained the war against his enemies for many years, and if in the end he lost the dominion of some cities, nevertheless he retained the kingdom.

Therefore, do not let our princes accuse fortune for the loss of their principalities after so many years' possession, but rather their own sloth, because in quiet times they never thought there could be a change (it is a common defect in man not to make any provision in the calm against the tempest), and when afterwards the bad times came they thought of flight and not of defending themselves, and they hoped that the people, disgusted with the insolence of the conquerors, would recall them. This course, when others fail, may be good, but it is very bad to have neglected all other expedients for that, since you would never wish to fall because you trusted to be able to find someone later on to restore you. This again either does not happen, or, if it does, it will not be for your security, because that deliverance is of no avail which does not depend upon yourself; those only are reliable, certain, and durable that depend on yourself and your valour.

The execution of Savonarola in 1498. The Dominican who had become leader of Florence in 1494 was pursued relentlessly by his enemies.

CHAPTER XXV

WHAT FORTUNE CAN EFFECT IN HUMAN AFFAIRS, AND HOW TO WITHSTAND HER

IT is not unknown to me how many men have had, and still have, the opinion that the affairs of the world are in such wise governed by fortune and by God that men with their wisdom cannot direct them and that no one can ever help them; and because of this they would have us believe that it is not necessary to labour much in affairs, but to let chance govern them. This opinion has been more credited in our times because of the great changes in affairs which have been seen, and may still be seen, every day, beyond all human conjecture. Sometimes pondering over this, I am in some degree inclined to their opinion. Nevertheless, not to extinguish our free will, I hold it to be true that Fortune is the arbiter of one half of our actions, but that she still leaves us to direct the other half, or perhaps a little less.

I compare her to one of those raging rivers, which when in flood overflows the plains, sweeping away trees and buildings, bearing away the soil from place to place; everything flies before it, all yield to its violence, without being able in any way to withstand it; and yet, though its nature be such, it does not follow therefore that men, when the weather becomes fair, shall not make provision, both with defences and barriers, in such a manner that, rising again, the waters may pass away by canal, and their force be neither so unrestrained nor so dangerous. So it happens with fortune, who shows her power where valour has not prepared to resist her, and thither she turns

This illuminated copy of Petrarch's Of Remedies for Fortune *shows Louis XII of France, who repeatedly laid claim to parts of Italy.*

her forces where she knows that barriers and defences have not been raised to constrain her.

And if you will consider Italy, which is the seat of these changes, and which has given to them their impulse, you will see it to be an open country without barriers and without any defence. For if it had been defended by proper valour, as are Germany, Spain, and France, either this invasion would not have made the great changes it has made or it would not have come at all. And this I consider enough to say concerning resistance to fortune in general.

But confining myself more to the particular, I say that a prince may be seen happy today and ruined tomorrow without having shown any change of disposition or character. This, I believe, arises firstly from causes that have already been discussed at length, namely, that the prince who relies entirely upon fortune is lost when it changes. I believe also that he will be successful who directs his actions according to the spirit of the times, and that he whose actions do not accord with the times will not be successful. Because men are seen, in affairs that lead to the end which every man has before him, namely, glory and riches, to get there by various methods; one with caution, another with haste; one by force, another by skill; one by patience, another by its opposite; and each one succeeds in reaching the goal by a different method. One can also see of two cautious men the one attain his end, the other fail; and similarly, two men by different observances are equally successful, the one being cautious, the other impetuous; all this arises from nothing else than whether or not they conform in their methods to the spirit of the times. This follows from what I have said, that two men working differently bring about the same effect, and of two working similarly, one attains his object and the other does not.

Changes in estate also issue from this, for if, to one who governs himself with caution and patience, times and affairs converge in such a way that his administration is successful, his fortune is made; but if times and affairs change, he is ruined if he does not change his course of action. But a man is not often found sufficiently circumspect to know how to accommodate himself to the change, both because he cannot deviate from what nature inclines him to, and also because, having always prospered by acting in one way, he cannot be persuaded that it is well to leave it; and, therefore, the cautious man, when it is time to turn adventurous, does not know how to do it, hence he is ruined; but had he changed his conduct with the times fortune would not have changed.

Pope Julius II went to work impetuously in all his affairs, and found the times and circumstances conformed so well to that line of action that he always met with success. Consider his first enterprise against Bologna, Messer Giovanni Bentivogli being still alive. The Venetians were not agreeable to it, nor was the king of Spain, and he had the enterprise still under discussion with the king of France; nevertheless he personally entered upon the expedition with his accustomed boldness and energy, a move which made Spain and the Venetians stand irresolute and passive, the latter from fear, the former from desire to recover all the kingdom of Naples; on the other hand, he drew after him the king of France, because that king, having observed the movement, and desiring to make the pope his friend so as to humble the Venetians, found it impossible to refuse him soldiers without manifestly offending him. Therefore Julius with his impetuous action accomplished what no other pontiff with simple human wisdom could have done; for if he had waited in Rome until he could get away, with his plans arranged and everything fixed, as any other pontiff would have done, he would never have succeeded. Because the king of France would have made a thousand excuses, and the others would have raised a thousand fears.

I will leave his other actions alone, as they were all alike, and they all succeeded, for the shortness of his life did not let him experience the contrary; but if circumstances had arisen which required him to go cautiously, his ruin would have followed, because he would never have deviated from those ways to which nature inclined him.

I conclude therefore that, fortune being changeful and mankind steadfast in their ways, so long as the two are in agreement men are successful, but unsuccessful when they fall out. For my part I consider that it is better to be adventurous than cautious, because fortune is a woman, and if you wish to keep her under it is necessary to beat and ill-use her; and it is seen that she allows herself to be mastered by the adventurous rather than by those who go to work more coldly. She is, therefore, always, woman-like, a lover of young men, because they are less cautious, more violent, and with more audacity command her.

The bronze doors from the fortress of Naples with the cannonball damage caused during the city's seizure in 1495 by Charles VIII.

CHAPTER XXVI

AN EXHORTATION TO LIBERATE AND SEIZE ITALY FROM THE BARBARIANS

HAVING carefully considered the subject of the above discourses, and wondering within myself whether the present times were propitious to a new prince, and whether there were the elements that would give an opportunity to a wise and virtuous one to introduce a new order of things which would do honour to him and good to the people of this country, it appears to me that so many things concur to favour a new prince that I never knew a time more fit than the present.

And if, as I said, it was necessary that the people of Israel should be captive so as to make manifest the ability of Moses; that the Persians should be oppressed by the Medes so as to discover the greatness of the soul of Cyrus; and that the Athenians should be dispersed to illustrate the capabilities of Theseus: then at the present time, in order to discover the virtue of an Italian spirit, it was necessary that Italy should be reduced to the extremity she is now in, that she should be more enslaved than the Hebrews, more oppressed than the Persians, more scattered than the Athenians; without head, without order, beaten, despoiled, torn, overrun; and to have endured every kind of desolation.

Although lately some spark may have been shown by one, which made us

---

The princely status of Lorenzo the Magnificent is accentuated in this fresco detail from the Medici palace chapel, Florence.

think he was ordained by God for our redemption, nevertheless it was afterwards seen, in the height of his career, that fortune rejected him; so that Italy, left as without life, waits for him who shall yet heal her wounds and put an end to the ravaging and plundering of Lombardy, to the swindling and taxing of the kingdom and of Tuscany, and cleanse those sores that for long have festered. It is seen how she entreats God to send someone who shall deliver her from these wrongs and barbarous insolencies. It is seen also that she is ready and willing to follow a banner if only someone will raise it.

Nor is there to be seen at present one in whom she can place more hope than in your illustrious house, with its valour and fortune, favoured by God and by the Church of which it is now the chief, and which could be made the head of this redemption. This will not be difficult if you will recall to yourself the actions and lives of the men I have named. And although they were great and wonderful men, yet they were men, and each one of them had no more opportunity than the present offers, for their enterprises were neither more just nor easier than this, nor was God more their friend than He is yours.

With us there is great justice, because that war is just which is necessary, and arms are hallowed when there is no other hope but in them. Here there is the greatest willingness, and where the willingness is great the difficulties cannot be great if you will only follow those men to whom I have directed your attention. Further than this, how extraordinarily the ways of God have been manifested beyond example: the sea is divided, a cloud has led the way, the rock has poured forth water, it has rained manna, everything has contributed to your greatness; you ought to do the rest. God is not willing to do everything, and thus take away our free will and that share of glory which belongs to us.

And it is not to be wondered at if none of the above-named Italians have been able to accomplish all that is expected from your illustrious house; and if in so many revolutions in Italy, and in so many campaigns, it has always appeared as if military strength were exhausted, this has happened because the old order of things was not good, and none of us have known how to find a new one. And nothing honours a man more than to establish new laws and new ordinances when he himself was newly risen. Such things when they are well founded and dignified will make him revered and admired, and in Italy there are not wanting opportunities to bring such into use in every form.

Here there is great valour in the limbs whilst it fails in the head. Look attentively at the duels and the hand-to-hand combats, how superior the Italians are in strength, dexterity, and subtlety. But when it comes to armies they do not bear comparison, and this springs entirely from the insufficiency of the leaders, since those who are capable are not obedient, and each one seems to himself to know, there having never been any one so distinguished above the rest, either by valour or fortune, that others would yield to him. Hence it is that for so long a time, and during so much fighting in the past twenty years, whenever there has been an army wholly Italian, it has always given a poor account of itself; as witness Il Taro, afterward Alexandria, Capua, Genoa, Vaila, Bologna, Mestri.

If, therefore, your illustrious house wishes to follow those remarkable men who have redeemed their country, it is necessary before all things, as a true foundation for every enterprise, to be provided with your own forces, because there can be no more faithful, truer, or better soldiers. And although singly they are good, altogether they will be much better when they find themselves commanded by their prince, honoured by him, and maintained at

his expense. Therefore it is necessary to be prepared with such arms, so that you can be defended against foreigners by Italian valour.

And although Swiss and Spanish infantry may be considered very formidable, nevertheless there is a defect in both, by reason of which a third order would not only be able to oppose them, but might be relied upon to overthrow them. For the Spaniards cannot resist cavalry, and the Switzers are afraid of infantry whenever they encounter them in close combat. Owing to this, as has been and may again be seen, the Spaniards are unable to resist French cavalry, and the Switzers are overthrown by Spanish infantry. And although a complete proof of this latter cannot be shown, nevertheless there was some evidence of it at the battle of Ravenna, when the Spanish infantry were confronted by German battalions, who follow the same tactics as the Swiss; when the Spaniards, by agility of body and with the aid of their shields, got in under the pikes of the Germans and stood out of danger, able to attack, while the Germans stood helpless, and, if the cavalry had not dashed up, all would have been over with them. It is possible, therefore, knowing the defects of both these infantries, to invent a new one, which will resist cavalry and not be afraid of infantry; this need not create a new order of arms, but a variation upon the old. And these are the kind of improvements which confer reputation and power upon a new prince.

This opportunity, therefore, ought not to be allowed to pass for letting Italy at last see her liberator appear. Nor can one express the love with which he would be received in all those provinces which have suffered so much from these foreign scourings, with what thirst for revenge, with what stubborn faith, with what devotion, with what tears. What door would be closed to him? Who would refuse obedience to him? What envy would hinder him?

What Italian would refuse him homage? To all of us this barbarous dominion stinks. Let, therefore, your illustrious house take up this charge with that courage and hope with which all just enterprises are undertaken, so that under its standard our native country may be ennobled, and under its auspices may be verified that saying of Petrarch:

Virtù contro al Furore
Prenderâ l'arme, e fia il combatter corto:
Che l'antico valore
Negli italici cuor non è ancor morto.[1]

NOTES FOR CHAPTER XXVI
[1] *Virtue against fury shall advance the fight,*
And the combat soon shall put to flight;
For the old Roman, valour is not dead,
Nor in th' Italians' breasts extinguished.
TRANSLATED BY EDWARD DACRE, 1640.

" M A C H I A V E L L I "

BY THOMAS BABINGTON MACAULAY
AN EDITED VERSION OF AN ESSAY FIRST PUBLISHED IN MARCH 1827

We doubt whether any name in literary history be so generally odious as that of the man whose character and writings we now propose to consider. The terms in which he is commonly described would seem to impart that he was the Tempter, the Evil Principle, the discoverer of ambition and revenge, the original inventor of perjury, and that, before the publication of his fatal *Prince*, there had never been a hypocrite, a tyrant, or a traitor, a simulated virtue, or a convenient crime. One writer gravely assures us that Maurice of Saxony learned all his fraudulent policy from that execrable volume. Another remarks, that, since it was translated into Turkish, the sultans have been more addicted than formerly to the custom of strangling their brothers. Lord Lyttelton charges the poor Florentine with the manifold treasons of the house of Guise, and with the Massacre of St. Bartholomew. Several authors have hinted that the Gunpowder Plot is to be primarily attributed to his doctrines, and seem to think that his effigy ought to be substituted for that of Guy Fawkes, in those processions by which the youth of England annually commemorate the preservation of the Three Estates. The Church of Rome has pronounced his works accursed things. Nor have our own countrymen been backward in testifying their opinion of his merits. Out of his surname they have coined an epithet for a knave, and out of his Christian name a synonym for the Devil.[1]

It is indeed scarcely possible for any person, not well acquainted with the history and literature of Italy, to read without horror and amazement the celebrated treatise which has brought so much obloquy on the name of Machiavelli. Such a display of wickedness, naked yet not ashamed, such cool, judicious, scientific atrocity, seemed rather to belong to a fiend than to the most depraved of men. Principles which the most hardened ruffian would scarcely hint to his most trusted accomplice, or avow, without the disguise of some palliating sophism, even to his own mind, are professed without the slightest circumlocution, and assumed as the fundamental axioms of all political science.

It is not strange that ordinary readers should regard the author of such a book as the most depraved and shameless of human beings. Wise men, however, have always been inclined to look with great suspicion on the angels and demons of the multitude; and, in the present instance, several circumstances have led even superficial observers to question the justice of the vulgar decision. It is notorious that Machiavelli was, through life, a zealous republican. In the same year in which he composed his manual of kingcraft, he suffered imprisonment and torture in the cause of public liberty. It seems inconceivable that the martyr of freedom should have designedly acted as the apostle of tyranny. Several eminent writers have, therefore, endeavored to detect in this unfortunate performance some concealed meaning, more consistent with the character and conduct of the author than that which appears at the first glance.

One hypothesis is that Machiavelli intended to practice on the young Lorenzo de Medici a fraud similar to that which Sunderland is said to have employed against our James II, and that he urged his pupil to violent and perfidious measures, as the surest means of accelerating the moment of deliverance and revenge. Another supposition which Lord Bacon seems to countenance, is that the treatise was merely a piece of grave irony, intended to warn nations against the arts of ambitious men. It would be easy to show that neither of these solutions is consistent with many passages in *The Prince* itself. But the most decisive refutation is that which is furnished by the other works of Machiavelli. In all the writings which he gave to the public, and in all those which the research of editors has, in the course of three centuries, discovered; in his comedies, designed for the entertainment of the multitude; in his comments on Livy, intended for the perusal of the most enthusiastic patriots of Florence; in his *History of Florence*, inscribed to one of the most amiable and estimable of the popes; in his public despatches; in his private memoranda, the same obliquity of moral principle for which *The Prince* is so severely censured is more or less discernible. We doubt whether it would be possible to find, in all the many volumes of his compositions, a single expression indicating that dissimulation and treachery had ever struck him as discreditable.

After this, it may seem ridiculous to say that we are acquainted with few writings which exhibit so much elevation of sentiment, so pure and warm a zeal for the public good, or so just a view of the duties and rights of citizens, as those of Machiavelli. Yet so it is. And even from *The Prince* itself we could select many passages in support of this remark. To a reader of our age and country, this inconsistency is, at first, perfectly bewildering. The whole man seems to be an enigma, a grotesque assemblage of incongruous qualities, selfishness and generosity, cruelty and benevolence, craft and simplicity, abject villany and romantic heroism. One sentence is such as a veteran diplomatist would scarcely write in cipher for the direction of his most confidential spy; the next seems to be extracted from a theme composed by an ardent school-boy on the death of Leonidas. An act of dexterous perfidy, and an act of patriotic self-devotion, call forth the same kind and the same degree of respectful admiration. The moral sensibility of the writer seems at once to be morbidly obtuse and morbidly acute. Two characters altogether dissimilar are united in him. They are not merely joined, but interwoven. They are the warp and the woof of his mind; and their combination, like that of the variegated threads in shot silk, gives to the whole texture a glancing and ever-changing appearance. The explanation might have been easy if he had been a very weak or a very affected man. But he was evidently neither the one nor the other. His works prove, beyond all contradiction, that his understanding was strong, his taste pure, and his sense of the ridiculous exquisitely keen.

This is strange, and yet the strangest is behind. There is no reason whatever to think that those amongst whom he lived saw anything shocking or incongruous in his writings. Abundant proofs remain of the high estimation in which both his works and his person were held by the most respectable among his contemporaries. Clement VII patronised the publication of those very books which the Council of Trent, in the following generation, pronounced unfit for the perusal of Christians. Some members of the democratical party censured the secretary for dedicating *The Prince* to a patron who bore the unpopular name of Medici. But to those immoral doctrines which have since called forth such severe reprehensions no exception appears to have been taken. The cry against them was first raised beyond the Alps, and seems to have been heard with amazement in Italy. The earliest assailant, as far as we are aware, was a countryman of our own, Cardinal Pole. The author of the *Anti-Machiavelli* was a French Protestant.

It is, therefore, in the state of moral feeling among the Italians of those times that we must seek for the real explanation of what seems most mysterious in the life and writings of this remarkable man. As this is a subject which suggests many interesting considerations, both political and metaphysical, we shall make no apology for discussing it at some length.

During the gloomy and disastrous centuries which followed the downfall of the Roman Empire, Italy had preserved, in a far greater degree than any other part of western Europe, the traces of ancient civilisation. The night which descended upon her was the night of an Arctic summer. The dawn began to reappear before the last reflection of the preceding sunset had faded from the horizon. It was in the time of the French Merovingians and of the Saxon Heptarchy that ignorance and ferocity seemed to have done their worst. Yet even then the Neapolitan provinces, recognising the authority of the Eastern Empire, preserved something of Eastern knowledge and refinement. Rome, protected by the sacred character of her pontiffs, enjoyed at least comparative security and repose. Even in those regions where the sanguinary Lombards had fixed their monarchy, there was incomparably more wealth, information, physical comfort and social order than could be found in Gaul, Britain, or Germany.

That which most distinguished Italy from the neighboring countries was the importance which the population of the towns, at a very early period, began to acquire. Some cities had been founded in wild and remote situations, by fugitives who had escaped from the rage of the barbarians. Such were Venice and Genoa, which preserved their freedom by their obscurity, till they became able to preserve it by their power. Other cities seem to have retained, under all the changing dynasties of invaders, under Odoacer and Theodoric, Narses and Alboin, the municipal institutions which had been conferred on them by the liberal policy of the Great Republic. In provinces which the central government was too feeble either to protect or to oppress, these institutions gradually acquired stability and vigor. The citizens, defended by their walls, and governed by their own magistrates and their own by-laws, enjoyed a considerable share of republican independence. Thus a strong democratic spirit was called into action. The Carlovingian sovereigns were too imbecile to subdue it. The generous policy of Otho encouraged it. It might perhaps have been suppressed by a close coalition between the Church and the empire. It was fostered and invigorated by their disputes. In the twelfth century it attained its full vigour, and, after a long and doubtful conflict, triumphed over the abilities and courage of the Swabian princes.

The assistance of the Ecclesiastical power had greatly contributed to the success of the Guelfs. That success would, however, have been a doubtful good, if its only effect had been to substitute a moral for a political servitude, and to exalt the popes at the expense of the Caesars. Happily the public mind of Italy had long contained the seeds of free opinions, which were now rapidly developed by the genial influence of free institutions. The people of that country had observed the whole machinery of the Church, its saints and its miracles, its lofty pretensions, and its splendid ceremonial, its worthless blessings and its harmless curses, too long and too closely to be duped. They stood behind the scenes on which others were gazing with childish awe and interest. They witnessed the arrangement of the pulleys, and the manufacture of the thunders. They saw the natural faces, and heard the natural voices, of the actors. Distant nations looked on the pope as the vicegerent of the Almighty, the oracle of the All-wise, the umpire from whose decisions, in the disputes either of theologians or of kings, no Christian ought to appeal. The Italians were acquainted with all the follies of his youth, and with all the dishonest arts by which he had attained power. They knew how often he had employed the keys of the Church to release himself from the most sacred engagements, and its wealth to pamper his mistresses and nephews. The doctrines and rites of the established religion they treated with decent reverence. But, though they still called themselves Catholics, they had ceased to be papists. Those spiritual arms which carried terror into the palaces and camps of the proudest sovereigns excited only contempt in the immediate neighborhood of the Vatican. Alexander, when he commanded our Henry II to submit to the lash before the tomb of a rebellious subject, was himself an exile. The Romans, apprehending that he entertained designs against their liberties, had driven him from their city; and, though he solemnly promised to confine himself for the future to his spiritual functions, they still refused to readmit him.

In every other part of Europe, a large and powerful privileged class trampled on the people and defied the government. But, in the most flourishing parts of Italy, the feudal nobles were reduced to comparative insignificance. In some districts they took shelter under the protection of the powerful commonwealths which they were unable to oppose, and gradually sank into the mass of burghers. In other places, they possessed great influence; but it was an influence widely different from that which was exercised by the aristocracy of any Transalpine kingdom. They were not petty princes, but eminent citizens. Instead of strengthening their fastnesses among the mountains, they embellished their palaces in the marketplace. The state of society in the Neapolitan dominions, and in some parts of the ecclesiastical state, more nearly resembled that which existed in the great monarchies of Europe. But the governments of Lombardy and Tuscany, through all their revolutions, preserved a different character. A people, when assembled in a town, is far more formidable to its rulers than when dispersed over a wide extent of country. The most arbitrary of the Caesars found it necessary to feed and divert the inhabitants of their unwieldy capital at the expense of the provinces. The citizens of Madrid have more than once besieged their sovereign in his own palace, and extorted from him the most humiliating concessions. The sultans have often been compelled to propitiate the furious rabble of Constantinople with the head of an unpopular vizier. From the same cause, there was a certain tinge of democracy in the monarchies and aristocracies of northern Italy.

Thus liberty, partially indeed and transiently, revisited Italy; and with liberty came commerce and empire, science and taste, all the comforts and all the ornaments of life. The Crusades, from which the inhabitants of other countries gained nothing but relics and wounds, brought to the rising commonwealths of the Adriatic and Tyrrhene seas a large increase of wealth, dominion, and knowledge. The moral and the geographical position of those commonwealths enabled them to profit alike by the barbarism of the West and by the civilisation of the East. Italian ships covered every sea. Italian factories rose on every shore. The tables of Italian money-changers were set in every city. Manufactures flourished. Banks were established. The operations of the commercial machine were facilitated by many useful and beautiful inventions. We doubt whether any country of Europe, our own excepted, has at the present time reached so high a point of wealth and civilisation as some parts of Italy had attained 400 years ago. Historians rarely descend to those details from which alone the real estate of a community can be collected. Hence posterity is too often deceived by the vague hyperboles of poets and rhetoricians, who mistake the splendor of a court for the happiness of a people. Fortunately, John Villani has given us an ample and precise account of the state of Florence in the early part of the fourteenth century. The revenue of the republic amounted to 300,000 florins, a sum which, allowing for the depreciation of the precious metals, was at least equivalent to 600,000 pounds sterling, a larger sum than England and Ireland, two centuries ago, yielded annually to Elizabeth. The manufacture of wool alone employed 200 factories and 30,000 workmen. The cloth annually produced sold, at an average, for 1,200,000 florins, a sum fully equal, in exchangeable value, to 2,500,000 pounds. Four hundred thousand florins were annually coined. Eighty banks conducted the commercial operations, not of Florence only, but of all Europe. The transactions of these establishments were sometimes of a magnitude which may surprise even the contemporaries of the Barings and the Rothschilds. Two houses advanced to Edward III of England upwards of 300,000 marks, at a time when the mark contained more silver than fifty shillings of the present day, and when the value of silver was more than quadruple what it is now. The city and its environs contained 170,000 inhabitants. In the various schools about 10,000 children were taught to read, 1,200 studied arithmetic, 600 received a learned education.

The progress of elegant literature and of the fine arts was proportioned to that of the public prosperity. Under the despotic successors of Augustus all the fields of the intellect had been turned into arid wastes, still marked out by formal boundaries, still retaining the traces of old cultivation, but yielding neither flowers nor fruit. The deluge of barbarism came. It swept away all the landmarks. It obliterated all the signs of former tillage. But, it fertilised while it devastated. When it receded, the wilderness was as the garden of God, rejoicing on every side, laughing, clapping its hands, pouring forth, in spontaneous abundance, every thing brilliant or fragrant or nourishing. A new language, characterised by simple sweetness and simple energy, had attained perfection. No tongue ever furnished more gorgeous and vivid tints to poetry; nor was it long before a poet appeared who knew how to employ them. Early in the fourteenth century came forth *The Divine Comedy*, beyond comparison the greatest work of imagination which had appeared since the poems of Homer. The following generation produced no second Dante, but it was eminently distinguished by general intellectual activity. The study of the Latin writers had never been wholly neglected in Italy. But Petrarch introduced a more profound, liberal, and elegant scholarship, and communicated to his countrymen that enthusiasm for the literature, the history, and the antiquities of Rome, which divided his own heart with a frigid mistress and a more frigid muse. Boccaccio turned their attention to the more sublime and graceful models of Greece.

From this time, the admiration of learning and genius became almost an idolatry among the people of Italy. Kings and republics, cardinals and doges, vied with each other in honoring and flattering Petrarch. Embassies from rival states solicited the honor of his instructions. His coronation agitated the court of Naples and the people of Rome as much as the most important political transaction could have done. To collect books and antiques, to found professorships, to patronise men of learning, became almost universal fashions among the great. The spirit of literary research allied itself to that of commercial enterprise. Every place to which the merchant princes of Florence extended their gigantic traffic, from the bazars of the Tigris to the monasteries of the Clyde, was ransacked for medals and manuscripts. Architecture, painting, and sculpture were munificently encouraged. Indeed, it would be difficult to name an Italian of eminence, during the period of which we speak, who, whatever may have been his general character, did not at least affect a love of letters and of the arts.

Knowledge and public prosperity continued to advance together. Both attained their meridian in the age of Lorenzo the Magnificent. . . . times in which the annals of England and France present us only with a frightful spectacle of poverty, barbarity, and ignorance. From the oppressions of illiterate masters, and the sufferings of a degraded peasantry, it is delightful to turn to the opulent and enlightened States of Italy, to the vast and magnificent cities, the ports, the arsenals, the villas, the museums, the libraries, the marts filled with every article of comfort or luxury, the factories swarming with artisans, the Apennines covered with rich cultivation up to their very summits, the Po wafting the harvests of Lombardy to the

granaries of Venice, and carrying back the silks of Bengal and
the furs of Siberia to the palaces of Milan. With peculiar pleasure every cultivated mind must repose on the fair, the happy,
the glorious Florence, the halls which rang with the mirth of
Pulci, the cell where twinkled the midnight lamp of Politian,
the statues on which the young eye of Michaelangelo glared
with the frenzy of a kindred inspiration, the gardens in which
Lorenzo meditated some sparkling song for the May-day dance
of the Etrurian virgins. Alas for the beautiful city! Alas for the
wit and the learning, the genius and the love!

"*Le donne, e i cavalieri, gli affanni e gli agi,*

Che ne'nvogliava amore e cortesia

Là dove i cuor son fatti sì malvagi."[2]

A time was at hand when all the seven vials of the
Apocalypse were to be poured forth and shaken out over those
pleasant countries, a time of slaughter, famine, beggary, infamy,
slavery, despair.

In the Italian States, as in many natural bodies, untimely
decrepitude was the penalty of precocious maturity. Their early
greatness, and their early decline, are principally to be attributed to the same cause – the preponderance which the towns
acquired in the political system.

In a community of hunters or of shepherds, every man easily and necessarily becomes a soldier. His ordinary avocations
are perfectly compatible with all the duties of military service.
However remote may be the expedition on which he is bound,
he finds it easy to transport with him the stock from which he
derives his subsistence. The whole people is an army; the whole
year a march. Such was the state of society which facilitated the
gigantic conquests of Attila and Tamerlane.

But a people which subsists by the cultivation of the earth
is in a very different situation. The husbandman is bound to the
soil on which he labours. A long campaign would be ruinous to
him. Still his pursuits are such as to give his frame both the active and the passive strength necessary to a soldier. Nor do they,
at least in the infancy of agricultural science, demand his unin-
terrupted attention. At particular times of the year he is almost

wholly unemployed, and can, without injury to himself, afford the time necessary for a short expedition. Thus the legions of Rome were supplied during its earlier wars. The season during which the fields did not require the presence of the cultivators sufficed for a short inroad and a battle. These operations, too frequently interrupted to produce decisive results, yet served to keep up among the people a degree of discipline and courage which rendered them, not only secure but formidable. The archers and billmen of the Middle Ages, who, with provisions for forty days at their backs, left the fields for the camp, were troops of the same description.

But when commerce and manufactures begin to flourish, a great change takes place. The sedentary habits of the desk and the loom render the exertions and hardships of war insupportable. The business of traders and artisans requires their constant presence and attention. In such a community there is little superfluous time; but there is generally much superfluous money. Some members of the society are, therefore, hired to relieve the rest from a task inconsistent with their habits and engagements.

The history of Greece is, in this, as in many other respects, the best commentary on the history of Italy. Five hundred years before the Christian era, the citizens of the republics round the Aegean Sea formed perhaps the finest militia that ever existed. As wealth and refinement advanced, the system underwent a gradual alteration. The Ionian States were the first in which commerce and the arts were cultivated, and the first in which the ancient discipline decayed. Within eighty years after the battle of Plataea, mercenary troops were everywhere plying for battles and sieges. In the time of Demosthenes, it was scarcely possible to persuade or compel the Athenians to enlist for foreign service. The laws of Lycurgus prohibited trade and manufactures. The Spartans, therefore, continued to form a national force long after their neighbors had begun to hire soldiers. But their military spirit declined with their singular institutions. In the second century before Christ, Greece contained only one nation of warriors, the savage highlanders of Aetolia, who were some generations behind their countrymen in civilisation and intelligence.

All the causes which produced these effects among the Greeks acted still more strongly on the modern Italians. Instead of a power like Sparta, in its nature warlike, they had amongst them an ecclesiastical state, in its nature pacific. Where there are numerous slaves, every freeman is induced by the strongest motives to familiarise himself with the use of arms. The commonwealths of Italy did not, like those of Greece, swarm with thousands of these household enemies. Lastly, the mode in which military operations were conducted during the prosperous times of Italy was peculiarly unfavorable to the formation of an efficient militia. Men covered with iron from head to foot, armed with ponderous lances, and mounted on horses of the largest breed, were considered as composing the strength of an army. The infantry was regarded as comparatively worthless, and was neglected till it became really so. These tactics maintained their ground for centuries in most parts of Europe. That foot soldiers could withstand the charge of heavy cavalry was thought utterly impossible, till, towards the close of the fifteenth century, the rude mountaineers of Switzerland dissolved the spell, and astounded the most experienced generals by receiving the dreaded shock on an impenetrable forest of pikes.

The use of the Grecian spear, the Roman sword, or the modern bayonet, might be acquired with comparative ease. But nothing short of the daily exercise of years could train the man at arms to support his ponderous panoply, and manage his unwieldy weapon. Throughout Europe this most important branch of war became a separate profession. Beyond the Alps, indeed, though a profession, it was not generally a trade. It was the duty and the amusement of a large class of country gentlemen. It was the service by which they held their lands, and the diversion by which, in the absence of mental resources, they beguiled their leisure. But in the northern states of Italy, as we have already remarked, the growing power of the cities, where it had not exterminated this order of men, had completely changed their habits. Here, therefore, the practice of employing mercenaries became universal, at a time when it was almost unknown in other countries.

When war becomes the trade of a separate class, the least dangerous course left to a government is to form that class into a standing army. It is scarcely possible that men can pass their lives in the service of one state without feeling some interest in its greatness. Its victories are their victories. Its defeats are their defeats. The contract loses something of its mercantile character. The services of the soldier are considered as the effects of patriotic zeal, his pay as the tribute of national gratitude. To betray the power which employs him, to be even remiss in its service, are in his eyes the most atrocious and degrading of crimes.

When the princes and commonwealths of Italy began to use hired troops, their wisest course would have been to form separate military establishments. Unhappily this was not done. The mercenary warriors of the peninsula, instead of being attached to the service of different powers, were regarded as the common property of all. The connection between the state and its defenders was reduced to the most simple and naked traffic. The adventurer brought his horse, his weapons, his strength, and his experience, into the market. Whether the king of Naples or the duke of Milan, the pope or the signory of Florence, struck the bargain, was to him a matter of perfect indifference. He was for the highest wages and the longest term. When the campaign for which he had contracted was finished, there was neither law nor punctilio to prevent him from instantly turning his arms against his late masters. The soldier was altogether disjoined from the citizen and from the subject.

The natural consequences followed. Left to the conduct of men who neither loved those whom they defended, nor hated those whom they opposed, who were often bound by stronger ties to the army against which they fought than to the state which they served, who lost by the termination of the conflict, and gained by its prolongation, war completely changed its character. Every man came into the field of battle impressed with the knowledge, that, in a few days, he might be taking the pay of the power against which he was then employed, and fighting by the side of his enemies against his associates. The strongest interests and the strongest feelings concurred to mitigate the hostility of those who had lately been brethren in arms, and who might soon be brethren in arms once more. Their common profession was a bond of union not to be forgotten, even when they were engaged in the service of contending parties. Hence it was that operations, languid and indecisive beyond any recorded in history, marches and counter-marches, pillaging expeditions and blockades, bloodless capitulations and equally bloodless combats, make up the military history of Italy during the course of nearly two centuries. Mighty armies fight from sunrise to sunset. A great victory is won. Thousands of prisoners are taken, and hardly a life is lost. A pitched battle seems to have been really less dangerous than an ordinary civil tumult.

Courage was now no longer necessary, even to the military character. Men grew old in camps, and acquired the highest renown by their warlike achievements, without being once required to face serious danger. The political consequences are too well known. The richest and most enlightened part of the world was left undefended to the assaults of every barbarous invader, to the brutality of Switzerland, the insolence of France, and the fierce rapacity of Aragon. The moral effects which followed from this state of things were still more remarkable.

Among the rude nations which lay beyond the Alps, valour was absolutely indispensable. Without it none could be eminent; few could be secure. Cowardice was, therefore, naturally considered as the foulest reproach. Among the polished Italians, enriched by commerce, governed by law, and passionately attached to literature, everything was done by superiority of intelligence. Their very wars, more pacific than the peace of their neighbors, required rather civil than military qualifications. Hence, while courage was the point of honor in other countries, ingenuity became the point of honor in Italy.

From these principles were deduced, by processes strictly analogous, two opposite systems of fashionable morality. Through the greater part of Europe, the vices which peculiarly belong to timid dispositions, and which are the natural defence of weakness, fraud, and hypocrisy, have always been most disreputable. On the other hand, the excesses of haughty and daring spirits have been treated with indulgence, and even with respect. The Italians regarded with corresponding lenity those crimes which require self-command, address, quick observation, fertile invention, and profound knowledge of human nature.

Such a prince as our Henry V would have been the idol of the North. The follies of his youth, the selfish ambition of his manhood, the Lollards roasted at slow fires, the prisoners massacred on the field of battle, the expiring lease of priestcraft renewed for another century, the dreadful legacy of a causeless and hopeless war bequeathed to a people who had no interest in its event – everything is forgotten but the victory of Agincourt. Francis Sforza, on the other hand, was the model of Italian heroes. He made his employers and his rivals alike his tools. He first overpowered his open enemies by the help of faithless allies; he then armed himself against his allies with the spoils taken from his enemies. By his incomparable dexterity, he raised himself from the precarious and dependent situation of a military adventurer to the first throne of Italy. To such a man much was forgiven, hollow friendship, ungenerous enmity, violated faith. Such are the opposite errors which men commit, when their morality is not a science, but a taste, when they abandon eternal principles for accidental associations.

We have illustrated our meaning by an instance taken from history. We will select another from fiction. Othello murders his wife; he gives orders for the murder of his lieutenant; he ends by murdering himself. Yet he never loses the esteem and affection of Northern readers. His intrepid and ardent spirit redeems everything. The unsuspecting confidence with which he listens to his adviser, the agony with which he shrinks from the thought of shame, the tempest of passion with which he commits his crimes, and the haughty fearlessness with which he avows them, give an extraordinary interest to his character. Iago, on the contrary, is the object of universal loathing. Many are inclined to suspect that Shakespeare has been seduced into an exaggeration unusual with him, and has drawn a monster who has no arche-type in human nature. Now we suspect that an Italian audience in the fifteenth century would have felt very differently. Oth-ello would have inspired nothing but detestation and contempt. The folly with which he trusts the friendly professions of a man whose promotion he had obstructed, the credulity with which he takes unsupported assertions, and trivial circumstances, for unanswerable proofs, the violence with which he silences the exculpation till the exculpation can only aggravate his misery, would have excited the abhorrence and disgust of his specta-tors. The conduct of Iago they would assuredly have condemned, but they would have condemned it as we condemn that of his victim. Something of interest and respect would have mingled with their disapprobation. The readiness of the traitor's wit, the clearness of his judgment, the skill with which he penetrates the dispositions of others, and conceals his own, would have insured to him a certain portion of their esteem.

So wide was the difference between the Italians and their neighbours. A similar difference existed between the Greeks of the second century before Christ, and their masters the Ro-mans. The conquerors, brave and resolute, faithful to their en-gagements, and strongly influenced by religious feelings, were, at the same time, ignorant, arbitrary, and cruel. With the van-quished people were deposited all the art, the science, and the literature of the Western world. In poetry, in philosophy, in painting, in architecture, in sculpture, they had no rivals. Their manners were polished, their perceptions acute, their inven-tion ready; they were tolerant, affable, humane; but of courage and sincerity they were almost utterly destitute. Every rude centurion consoled himself for his intellectual inferiority, by remarking that knowledge and taste seemed only to make men atheists, cowards and slaves. The distinction long continued to be strongly marked, and furnished and admirable subject for the fierce sarcasms of Juvenal.

The citizen of an Italian commonwealth was the Greek of the time of Juvenal and the Greek of the time of Pericles, joined in one. Like the former, he was timid and pliable, artful and mean. But, like the latter, he had a country. Its independence and prosperity were dear to him. If his character were degraded by some base crimes, it was, on the other hand, ennobled by public spirit and by an honorable ambition.

A vice sanctioned by the general opinion is merely a vice. The evil terminates in itself. A vice condemned by the general opinion produces a pernicious effect on the whole character. The former is a local malady, the latter a constitutional taint. When the reputation of the offender is lost, he, too, often flings the remains of his virtue after it in despair. The Highland gentleman, who, a century ago, lived by taking blackmail from his neighbours, committed the same crime for which [Jonathan] Wild was accompanied to Tyburn by the huzzas of 200,000 people.[3] But there can be no doubt that he was a much less depraved man than Wild. The deed for which Mrs Brownrigg was hanged, sinks into nothing when compared with the conduct of the Roman who treated the public to 100 pairs of gladiators. Yet we should greatly wrong such a Roman if we supposed that his disposition was as cruel as that of Mrs Brownrigg. In our own country, a woman forfeits her place in society by what, in a man, is too commonly considered as an honorable distinction, and at worst as a venial error. The consequence is notorious. The moral principle of a woman is frequently more impaired by a single lapse from virtue than that of a man by twenty years of intrigues. Classical antiquity would furnish us with instances stronger, if possible, than those to which we have referred.

We must apply this principle to the case before us. Habits of dissimulation and falsehood, no doubt, mark a man of our age and country as utterly worthless and abandoned. But it by no means follows that a similar judgment would be just in the case of an Italian in the Middle Ages. On the contrary, we frequently find those faults which we are accustomed to consider as certain indications of a mind altogether depraved, in company with great and good qualities, with generosity, with benevolence, with disinterestedness. From such a state of society, Palamedes, in the admirable dialogue of Hume, might have drawn illustrations of his theory as striking as any of those with which Fourli furnished him. These are not, we well know, the lessons which historians are generally most careful to teach, or readers most willing to learn. But they are not therefore useless. How Philip disposed his troops at Chaeronea, where Hannibal crossed the Alps, whether Mary blew up Darnley, or Siquier shot Charles XII, and the ten thousand other questions of the same description, are in themselves unimportant. The inquiry may amuse us, but the decision leaves us no wiser. He alone reads history aright, who, observing how powerfully circumstances influence the feelings and opinions of men, how often vices pass into virtues, and paradoxes into axioms, learns to distinguish what is accidental and transitory in human nature, from what is essential and immutable.

In this respect, no history suggests more important reflections than that of the Tuscan and Lombard commonwealths. The character of the Italian statesman seems, at first sight, a collection of contradictions, a phantom as monstrous as the portress of hell in Milton, half divinity, half snake, majestic and beautiful above, grovelling and poisonous below. We see a man whose thoughts and words have no connection with each other, who never hesitates at an oath when he wishes to seduce, who never wants a pretext when he is inclined to betray. His cruelties spring, not from the heat of blood, or the insanity of uncontrolled power, but from deep and cool meditation. His passions, like well-trained troops, are impetuous by rule, and in their most headstrong fury never forget the discipline to which they have been accustomed. His whole soul is occupied with vast and complicated schemes of ambition, yet his aspect and language exhibit nothing but philosophical moderation. Hatred and revenge eat into his heart; yet every look is a cordial smile, every gesture a familiar caress. He never excites the suspicion of his adversaries by petty provocations. His purpose is disclosed only when it is accomplished. His face is unruffled, his speech is courteous, till vigilance is laid asleep, till a vital point is exposed, till a sure aim is taken; and then he strikes for the first and last time. Military courage, the boast of the sottish German, of the frivolous and prating Frenchman, of the romantic and arrogant Spaniard, he neither possesses nor values. He shuns danger, not because he is insensible to shame, but because, in the society in which he lives, timidity has ceased to be shameful. To do an injury openly is, in his estimation, as wicked as to do it secretly, and far less profitable. With him the most honorable means are those which are the surest, the speediest, and the darkest. He cannot comprehend how a man should scruple to deceive those whom he does not scruple to destroy. He would think it madness to declare open hostilities against rivals whom he might stab in a friendly embrace, or poison in a consecrated wafer.

Yet this man, black with the vices which we consider as most loathsome, traitor, hypocrite, coward, assassin, was by no means destitute even of those virtues which we generally consider as indicating superior elevation of character. In civil courage, in perseverance, in presence of mind, those barbarous warriors, who were foremost in the battle or the breach, were far his inferiors. Even the dangers which he avoided with a caution almost pusillanimous never confused his perceptions, never paralyzed his inventive faculties, never wrung out one secret from his smooth tongue and his inscrutable brow. Though a dangerous enemy, and a still more dangerous accomplice, he could be a just and beneficent ruler. With so much unfairness in his policy, there was an extraordinary degree of fairness in his intellect. Indifferent to truth in the transactions of life, he was honestly devoted to truth in the researches of speculation. Wanton cruelty was not in his nature. On the contrary, where no political object was at stake, his disposition was soft and humane. The susceptibility of his nerves and the activity of his imagination inclined him to sympathise with the feelings of others, and to delight in the charities and courtesies of social life. Perpetually descending to actions which might seem to mark a mind diseased through all its faculties, he had nevertheless an exquisite sensibility, both for the natural and the moral sublime, for every graceful and every lofty conception. Habits of petty intrigue and dissimulation might have rendered him incapable of great general views, but that the expanding effect of his philosophical studies counteracted the narrowing tendency. He had the keenest enjoyment of wit, eloquence, and poetry. The fine arts profited alike by the severity of his judgment, and by the liberality of his patronage. The portraits of some of the remarkable Italians of those times are perfectly in harmony with this description. Ample and majestic foreheads; brows strong and dark, but not frowning; eyes of which the calm, full gaze, while it expresses nothing, seems to discern everything; cheeks pale with thought and sedentary habits; lips formed with feminine delicacy, but compressed with more than masculine decision-mark out men at once enterprising and timid, men equally skilled in detecting the purposes of others, in and concealing their own, men who must have been formidable enemies and unsafe allies, but men, at the same time, whose tempers were mild and equable, and who possessed an amplitude and subtlety of intellect which would have rendered them eminent either in active or in contemplative life, and fitted them either to govern or to instruct mankind.

Every age and every nation has certain characteristic vices, which prevail almost universally, which scarcely any person scruples to avow, and which even rigid moralists but faintly censure. Succeeding generations change the fashion of their morals, with the fashion of their hats and their coaches; take some other kind of wickedness under their patronage, and wonder at the depravity of their ancestors. Nor is this all. Posterity, that high court of appeal which is never tired of eulogising its own justice and discernment, acts on such occasions like a Roman dictator after a general mutiny. Finding the delinquents too numerous to be all punished, it selects some of them at hazard, to bear the whole penalty of an offence in which they are not more deeply implicated than those who escape. Whether decimation be a convenient mode of military execution, we know not; but we solemnly protest against the introduction of such a principle into the philosophy of history.

In the present instance, the lot has fallen on Machiavelli, a man whose public conduct was upright and honorable, whose views of morality, where they differed from those of the persons around him, seemed to have differed for the better, and whose only fault was, that, having adopted some of the maxims then generally received, he arranged them more luminously, and expressed them more forcibly, than any other writer.[4]

The political correspondence of Machiavelli, first published in 1767, is unquestionably genuine, and highly valuable. The unhappy circumstances in which his country was placed during the greater part of his public life gave extraordinary encouragement to diplomatic talents. From the moment that Charles VIII descended from the Alps the whole character of Italian politics was changed. The governments of the peninsula ceased to form an independent system. Drawn from their old orbit by the attraction of the larger bodies which now approached them, they became mere satellites of France and Spain. All their disputes, internal and external, were decided by foreign influence. The contests of opposite factions were carried on, not as formerly in the senate-house or in the marketplace, but in the ante-chambers of Louis and Ferdinand. Under these circumstances, the prosperity of the Italian States depended far more on the ability of their foreign agents, than on the conduct of those who were intrusted with the domestic administration. The ambassador had to discharge functions far more delicate than transmitting orders of knighthood, introducing tourists, or presenting his brethren with the homage of his high consideration. He was an advocate to whose management the dearest interests of his clients were intrusted, a spy clothed with an inviolable character. Instead of consulting, by a reserved manner and ambiguous style, the dignity of those whom he represented, he was to plunge into all the intrigues of the court at which he resided, to discover and flatter every weakness of the prince, and of the favourite who governed the prince, and of the lackey who governed the favourite. He was to compliment the mistress, and bribe the confessor, to panegyrize or supplicate, to laugh or weep, to accommodate himself to every caprice, to lull every suspicion, to treasure every hint, to be every thing, to observe every thing, to endure every thing. High as the art of political intrigue had been carried in Italy, these were times which required it all.

On these arduous errands Machiavelli was frequently employed. He was sent to treat with the King of the Romans and with the Duke of Valentinois. He was twice ambassador at the Court of Rome, and thrice at that of France. In these missions, and in several others of inferior importance, he acquitted himself with great dexterity. His despatches form one of the most amusing and instructive collections extant. The narratives are clear and agreeably written, the remarks on men and things clever and judicious. The conversations are reported in a spirited and characteristic manner. We find ourselves introduced into the presence of the men who, during twenty eventful years, swayed the destinies of Europe. Their wit and their folly, their fretfulness and their merriment, are exposed to us. We are admitted to overhear their chat, and to watch their familiar gestures. It is interesting and curious to recognise, in circumstances which elude the notice of historians, the feeble violence and shallow cunning of Louis XII; the bustling insignificance of Maximilian, cursed with an impotent pruriency for renown, rash yet timid, obstinate yet fickle, always in a hurry, yet always too late; the fierce and haughty energy which gave dignity to the eccentricities of Julius; the soft and graceful manners which masked the insatiable ambition and the implacable hatred of Caesar Borgia.

We have mentioned Caesar Borgia. It is impossible not to pause for a moment on the name of a man in whom the political morality of Italy was so strongly personified, partially blended with the sterner lineaments of the Spanish character. On two important occasions Machiavelli was admitted to his society — once, at the moment when Caesar's splendid villainy achieved its most signal triumph, when he caught in one snare, and crushed at one blow, all his most formidable rivals; and again when, exhausted by disease and overwhelmed by misfortunes, which no human prudence could have averted, he was the prisoner of the deadliest enemy of his house. These interviews between the greatest speculative and the greatest practical statesmen of the age are fully described in the *Correspondence*, and form perhaps the most interesting part of it. From some passages in *The Prince*, and perhaps also from some indistinct traditions, several writers have supposed a connection between those remarkable men much closer than ever existed. The envoy has even been accused of prompting the crimes of the artful and merciless tyrant. But, from the official documents, it is clear that their intercourse, though ostensibly amicable, was in reality hostile. It cannot be doubted, however, that the imagination of Machiavelli was strongly impressed, and his speculations on government coloured, by the observations which he made on the singular character and equally singular fortunes of a man who under such disadvantages had achieved such exploits; who, when sensuality, varied through innumerable forms, could no longer stimulate his sated mind, found a more powerful and durable excitement in the intense thirst of empire and revenge; who emerged from the sloth and luxury of the Roman purple the first prince and general of the age; who, trained in an unwarlike profession, formed a gallant army out of the dregs of an unwarlike people; who, after acquiring sovereignty by destroying his enemies, acquired popularity by destroying his tools; who had begun to employ for the most salutary ends the power which he had attained by the most atrocious means; who tolerated within the sphere of his iron despotism no plunderer or oppressor but himself; and who fell at last amidst the mingled curses and regrets of a people of whom his genius had been the wonder, and might have been the salvation. Some of those crimes of Borgia which to us appear the most odious would not, from causes which we have already considered, have struck an Italian of the fifteenth century with equal horror. Patriotic feeling also might induce Machiavelli to look with some indulgence and regret on the memory of the only leader who could have defended the independence of Italy against the confederate spoilers of Cambray.

On this subject Machiavelli felt most strongly. Indeed, the expulsion of the foreign tyrants, and the restoration of that golden age which had preceded the irruption of Charles VIII, were projects which, at that time, fascinated all the master-spirits of Italy. The magnificent vision delighted the great but ill-regulated mind of Julius. It divided with manuscripts and saucers, painters and falcons, the attention of the frivolous Leo. It prompted the generous treason of Morone. It imparted a transient energy to the feeble mind and body of the last Sforza. It excited for one moment an honest ambition in the false heart of Pescara. Ferocity and insolence were not among the vices of the national character. To the discriminating cruelties of politicians, committed for great ends on select victims, the moral code of the Italians was too indulgent. But, though they might have recourse to barbarity as an expedient, they did not require it as a stimulant. They turned with loathing from the atrocity of the strangers who seemed to love blood for its own sake; who, not content with subjugating, were impatient to destroy; who found a fiendish pleasure in razing magnificent cities, cutting the throats of enemies who cried for quarter, or suffocating an unarmed population by thousands in the caverns to which it had fled for safety. Such were the cruelties which daily excited the terror and disgust of a people among whom, till lately, the worst that a soldier had to fear in a pitched battle was the loss of his horse and the expense of his ransom. The swinish intemperance of Switzerland, the wolfish avarice of Spain, the gross licentiousness of the French, indulged in violation of hospitality, of decency, of love itself, the wanton inhumanity which was common to all the invaders had made them objects of deadly hatred to the inhabitants of the peninsula. The wealth which had been accumulated during centuries of prosperity and repose was rapidly melting away. The intellectual superiority of the oppressed people only rendered them more keenly sensible of their political degradation. Literature and taste, indeed, still disguised with a flush of hectic loveliness and brilliancy the ravages of an incurable decay. The iron had not yet entered into the soul. The time was not yet come when eloquence was to be gagged, and reason to be hoodwinked, when the harp of the poet was to be hung on the willows of Arno, and the right hand of the painter to forget its cunning. Yet a discerning eye might even then have seen that genius and learning would not long survive the state of things from which they had sprung, and that the great men whose talents gave lustre to that melancholy period had been formed under the influence of happier days, and would leave no successors behind them. The times which shine with the greatest splendor in literary history are not always those to which the human mind is most indebted. Of this we may be convinced, by comparing the generation which follows them with that which had preceded them. The first fruits which are reaped under a bad system often spring from seed sown under a good one. Thus it was, in some measure, with the Augustan age. Thus it was with the age of Raphael and Ariosto, of Aldus and Vida.

Machiavelli deeply regretted the misfortunes of his country, and clearly discerned the cause and the remedy. It was the military system of the Italian people which had extinguished their valor and discipline, and left their wealth an easy prey to every foreign plunderer. The secretary projected a scheme, alike honourable to his heart and to his intellect, for abolishing the use of mercenary troops, and for organising a national militia.

The exertions which he made to effect this great object ought alone to rescue his name from obloquy. Though his situation and his habits were pacific, he studied with intense assiduity the theory of war. He made himself master of all its details. The Florentine government entered into his views. A council of war was appointed. Levies were decreed. The indefatigable minister flew from place to place in order to superintend the execution of his design. The times were, in some respects, favourable to the experiment. The system of military tactics had undergone a great revolution. The cavalry was no longer considered as forming the strength of an army. The hours which a citizen could spare from his ordinary employments, though by no means sufficient to familiarise him with the exercise of a man-at-arms, might render him a useful foot-soldier. The dread of a foreign yoke, of plunder, massacre, and conflagration, might have conquered that repugnance to military pursuits which both the industry and the idleness of great towns commonly generate. For a time the scheme promised well. The new troops acquitted themselves respectably in the field.

Machiavelli looked with parental rapture on the success of his plan, and began to hope that the arms of Italy might once more be formidable to the barbarians of the Tagus and the Rhine. But the tide of misfortune came on before the barriers which should have withstood it were prepared. For a time, indeed, Florence might be considered as peculiarly fortunate. Famine and sword and pestilence had devastated the fertile plains and stately cities of the Po. All the curses denounced of old against Tyre seemed to have fallen on Venice. Her merchants already stood afar off, lamenting for their great city. The time seemed near when the seaweed should overgrow her silent Rialto, and the fisherman wash his nets in her deserted arsenal. Naples had been four times conquered and reconquered by tyrants equally indifferent to its welfare, and equally greedy for its spoils. Florence, as yet, had only to endure degradation and extortion, to submit to the mandates of foreign powers, to buy over and over again, at an enormous price, what was already justly her own, to return thanks for being wronged, and to ask pardon for being in the right. She was at length deprived of the blessings even of this infamous and servile repose. Her military and political institutions were swept away together. The Medici returned, in the train of foreign invaders, from their long exile. The policy of Machiavelli was abandoned; and his public services were requited with poverty, imprisonment, and torture.

The fallen statesman still clung to his project with unabated ardour. With the view of vindicating it from some popular objections, and of refuting some prevailing errors on the subject of military science, he wrote his *The Art of War*. This excellent work is in the form of a dialogue. The opinions of the writer are put into the mouth of Fabrizio Colonna, a powerful nobleman of the ecclesiastical state, and an officer of distinguished merit in the service of the king of Spain. Colonna visits Florence on his way from Lombardy to his own domains. He is invited to meet some friends at the house of Cosimo Rucellai, an amiable and accomplished young man, whose early death Machiavelli feelingly deplores. After partaking of an elegant entertainment, they retire from the heat into the most shady recesses of the garden. Fabrizio is struck by the sight of some uncommon plants. Cosimo says that, though rare, in modern days, they are frequently mentioned by the classical authors, and that his grandfather, like many other Italians, amused himself with practising the ancient methods of gardening. Fabrizio expresses his regret that those who, in later times, affected the manners of the old Romans, should select for imitation the most trifling pursuits. This leads to a conversation on the decline of military discipline and on the best means of restoring it. The institution of the Florentine militia is ably defended, and several improvements are suggested in the details.

The Swiss and the Spaniards were, at that time, regarded as the best soldiers in Europe. The Swiss battalion consisted of pikemen, and bore a close resemblance to the Greek phalanx. The Spaniards, like the soldiers of Rome, were armed with the sword and the shield. The victories of Flamininus and Aemilius over the Macedonian kings seem to prove the superiority of the weapons used by the legions. The same experiment had been recently tried with the same result at the battle of Ravenna, one of those tremendous days into which human folly and wickedness compress the whole devastation of a famine or a plague. In that memorable conflict, the infantry of Aragon, the old companions of Gonsalvo, deserted by all their allies, hewed a passage through the thickest of the imperial pikes, and effected an unbroken retreat, in the face of the gendarmerie of De Foix, and the renowned artillery of Este. Fabrizio, or rather Machiavelli, proposes to combine the two systems, to arm the foremost lines with the pike for the purpose of repulsing cavalry, and those in the rear with the sword, as being a weapon better adapted for every other purpose. Throughout the work, the author expresses the highest admiration of the military science of the ancient Romans, and the greatest contempt for the maxims which had been in vogue amongst the Italian commanders of the preceding generation. He prefers infantry to cavalry, and fortified camps to fortified towns. He is inclined to substitute rapid movements and decisive engagements for the languid and dilatory operations of his countrymen. He attaches very little importance to the invention of gunpowder. Indeed, he seems to think that it ought scarcely to produce any change in the mode of arming or of disposing troops. The general testimony of historians, it must be allowed, seems to prove that the ill-constructed and ill-served artillery of those times, though useful in a siege, was of little value on the field of battle.

Of the tactics of Machiavelli we will not venture to give an opinion, but we are certain that his book is most able and interesting. As a commentary on the history of his times, it is invaluable. The ingenuity, the grace, and the perspicuity of the style, and the eloquence and animation of particular passages, must give pleasure, even to readers who take no interest in the subject.

The Prince and the *Discourses on Livy* were written after the fall of the republican government. The former was dedicated to the young Lorenzo de' Medici. This circumstance seems to have disgusted the contemporaries of the writer far more that the doctrines which have rendered the name of the work odious in later times. It was considered as an indication of political apostasy. The fact, however, seems to have been that Machiavelli, despairing of the liberty of Florence, was inclined to support any government which might preserve her independence. The interval which separated a democracy and a despotism, Soderini and Lorenzo, seemed to vanish when compared with the difference between the former and the present state of Italy, between the security, the opulence, and the repose which she had enjoyed under its native rulers, and the misery in which she had been plunged since the fatal year in which the first foreign tyrant had descended from the Alps. The noble and pathetic exhortation with which *The Prince* concludes shows how strongly the writer felt upon this subject.

The Prince traces the progress of an ambitious man, the *Discourses* the progress of an ambitious people. The same principles on which, in the former work, the elevation of an individual is explained, are applied in the latter, to the longer duration and more complex interest of a society. To a modern statesman the form of the *Discourses* may appear to be puerile. In truth, Livy is not a historian on whom implicit reliance can be placed, even in cases where he must have possessed considerable means of information. And the first Decade, to which Machiavelli has confined himself, is scarcely entitled to more credit than our chronicle of British kings who reigned before the Roman invasion. But the commentator is indebted to Livy for little more than a few texts which he might as easily have extracted from the Vulgate or *The Decameron*. The whole train of thought is original.

On the peculiar immorality which has rendered *The Prince* unpopular, and which is almost equally discernible in the *Discourses*, we have already given our opinion at length. We have attempted to show that it belonged rather to the age than to the man, that it was a partial taint, and by no means implied general depravity. We cannot, however, deny that it is a great blemish, and that it considerably diminishes the pleasure which, in other respects, those works must afford to every intelligent mind.

It is, indeed, impossible to conceive a more healthful and vigorous constitution of the understanding than that which these works indicate. The qualities of the active and the contemplative statesman appear to have been blended in the mind of the writer into a rare and exquisite harmony. His skill in the details of business had not been acquired at the expense of his general powers. It had not rendered his mind less comprehensive; but it had served to correct his speculations, and to impart to them that vivid and practical character which so widely distinguishes them from the vague theories of most political philosophers.

Every man who has seen the world knows that nothing is so useless as a general maxim. If it be very moral and very true, it may serve for a copy to a charity boy. If, like those of Rochefoucault, it be sparkling and whimsical, it may make an excellent motto for an essay. But few indeed of the many wise apophthegms which have been uttered, from the time of the Seven Sages of Greece to that of Poor Richard, have prevented a single foolish action. We give the highest and the most peculiar praise to the precepts of Machiavelli when we say that they may frequently be of real use in regulating conduct, not so much because they are more just or more profound than those which might be culled from other authors, as because they can be more readily applied to the problems of real life.

There are errors in these works. But they are errors which a writer, situated like Machiavelli, could scarcely avoid. They arise, for the most part, from a single defect which appears to us to pervade his whole system. In his political scheme, the means had been more deeply considered than the ends. The great principle, that societies and laws exist only for the purpose of increasing the sum of private happiness, is not recognised with sufficient clearness. The good of the body, distinct from the good of the members, and sometimes hardly compatible with the good of the members, seems to be the object which he proposes to himself. Of all political fallacies, this has perhaps had the widest and the most mischievous operation. The state of society in the little commonwealths of Greece, the close connection and mutual dependence of the citizens, and the severity of the laws of war, tended to encourage an opinion which, under such circumstances, could hardly be called erroneous. The interests of every individual were inseparably bound up with those of the state. An invasion destroyed his cornfields and vineyards, drove him from his home, and compelled him to encounter all the hardships of a military life. A treaty of peace restored him to security and comfort. A victory doubled the number of his slaves. A defeat perhaps made him a slave himself. When Pericles, in the Peloponnesian war, told the Athenians, that, if their country triumphed, their private losses would speedily be repaired, but that, if their arms failed of success, every individual amongst them would probably be ruined, he spoke no more than the truth. He spoke to men whom the tribute of vanquished cities supplied with food and clothing, with the luxury of the bath and the amusements of the theatre, on whom the greatness of their country conferred rank, and before whom the members of less prosperous communities trembled; to men who, in case of a change in the public fortunes, would, at least, be deprived of every comfort and every distinction which they enjoyed. To be butchered on the smoking ruins of their city, to be dragged in chains to a slave market, to see one child torn from them to dig in the quarries of Sicily, and another to guard the harems of Persepolis, these were the frequent and probable consequences of national calamities. Hence, among the Greeks, patriotism became a governing principle, or rather an ungovernable passion. Their legislators and their philosophers took it for granted that, in providing for the strength and greatness of the state, they sufficiently provided for the happiness of the people. The writers of the Roman Empire lived under despots, into whose dominion a hundred nations were melted down, and whose gardens would have covered the little commonwealths of Phlius and Plataea. Yet they continued to employ the same language, and to cant about the duty of sacrificing everything to a country to which they owed nothing.

Causes similar to those which had influenced the disposition of the Greeks operated powerfully on the less vigorous and daring character of the Italians. The Italians, like the Greeks, were members of small communities. Every man was deeply interested in the welfare of the society to which he belonged, a partaker in its wealth and its poverty, in its glory and its shame. In the age of Machiavelli this was peculiarly the case. Public events had produced an immense sum of misery to private citizens. The Northern invaders had brought want to their boards, infamy to their beds, fire to their roofs, and the knife to their throats. It was natural that a man who lived in times like these should overrate the importance of those measures by which a nation is rendered formidable to its neighbours, and undervalue those which make it prosperous within itself.

Nothing is more remarkable in the political treatises of Machiavelli than the fairness of mind which they indicate. It appears where the author is in the wrong, almost as strongly as where he is in the right. He never advances a false opinion because it is new or splendid, because he can clothe it in a happy phrase, or defend it by an ingenious sophism. His errors are at once explained by a reference to the circumstances in which he was placed. They evidently were not sought out: they lay in his way, and could scarcely be avoided. Such mistakes must necessarily be committed by early speculators in every science.

Propriety of thought, and propriety of diction, are commonly found together. Obscurity and affectation are the two greatest faults of style. Obscurity of expression generally springs from confusion of ideas; and the same wish to dazzle at any cost which produces affectation in the manner of a writer is likely to produce sophistry in his reasonings. The judicious and candid mind of Machiavelli shows itself in his luminous, manly, and polished language.

The political works of Machiavelli derive a peculiar interest from the mournful earnestness which he manifests whenever he touches on topics connected with the calamities of his native land. It is difficult to conceive any situation more painful than that of a great man, condemned to watch the lingering agony of an exhausted country, to tend it during the alternate fits of stupefaction and raving which precede its dissolution, and to see the symptoms of vitality disappear one by one, till nothing is left but coldness, darkness, and corruption. To this joyless and thankless duty was Machiavelli called. In the energetic language of the prophet, he was "mad for the sight of his eyes which he saw" – disunion in the Council, effeminacy in the camp, liberty extinguished, commerce decaying, national honor sullied, an enlightened and flourishing people given over to the ferocity of ignorant savages. Though his opinions had not escaped the contagion of that political immorality which was common among his countrymen, his natural disposition seems to have been rather stern and impetuous than pliant and artful. When the misery and degradation of Florence, and the foul outrage which he had himself sustained, recur to his mind, the smooth craft of his profession and his nation is exchanged for the honest bitterness of scorn and anger. He speaks like one sick of the calamitous times and abject people among whom his lot is cast. He pines for the strength and glory of ancient Rome, for the fasces of Brutus and the sword of Scipio, the gravity of the curule chair, and the bloody pomp of the triumphal sacrifice.

He seems to be transported back to the days when 800,000 Italian warriors sprung to arms at the rumour of a Gallic invasion. He breathes all the spirit of those intrepid and haughty senators who forgot the dearest ties of nature in the claims of public duty, who looked with disdain on the elephants and on the gold of Pyrrhus, and listened with unaltered composure to the tremendous tidings of Cannae. Like an ancient temple deformed by the barbarous architecture of a later age, his character acquires an interest from the very circumstances which debase it. The original proportions are rendered more striking by the contrast which they present to the mean and incongruous additions.

The influence of the sentiments which we have described was not apparent in his writings alone. His enthusiasm, barred from the career which it would have selected for itself, seems to have found a vent in desperate levity. He enjoyed a vindictive pleasure in outraging the opinions of a society which he despised. He became careless of the decencies which were expected from a man so highly distinguished in the literary and political world. The sarcastic bitterness of his conversation disgusted those who were more inclined to accuse his licentiousness than their own degeneracy, and who were unable to conceive the strength of those emotions which are concealed by the jests of the wretched, and by the follies of the wise.

The historical works of Machiavelli still remain to be considered. The life of Castruccio Castracani will occupy us for a very short time, and would scarcely have demanded our notice had it not attracted a much greater share of public attention than it deserves. Few books, indeed, could be more interesting than a careful and judicious account, from such a pen, of the illustrious Prince of Lucca, the most eminent of those Italian chiefs, who, like Pisistratus and Gelon, acquired a power felt rather than seen, and resting, not on law or on prescription, but on the public favor and on their great personal qualities. Such a work would exhibit to us the real nature of that species of sovereignty, so singular and so often misunderstood, which the Greeks denominated tyranny, and which, modified in some degree by the feudal system, reappeared in the commonwealths of Lombardy and Tuscany. But this little composition of Machiavelli is in no sense a history. It has no pretensions to fidelity. It is trifle, and not a very successful trifle. It is scarcely more authentic than the novel of *Belphegor*,[5] and is very much duller.

The last great work of this illustrious man was the history of his native city. It was written by command of the pope, who, as chief of the house of Medici, was at that time sovereign of Florence. The characters of Cosimo, of Piero, and of Lorenzo, are, however, treated with a freedom and impartiality equally honorable to the writer and to the patron. The miseries and humiliations of dependence, the bread which is more bitter than every other food, the stairs which are more painful than every other ascent, had not broken the spirit of Machiavelli. The most corrupting post in a corrupting profession had not depraved the generous heart of Clement.

The *History of Florence* does not appear to be the fruit of much industry or research. It is unquestionably inaccurate. But it is elegant, lively, and picturesque, beyond any other in the Italian language. The reader, we believe, carries away from it a more vivid and a more faithful impression of the national character and manners than from more correct accounts. The truth is, that the book belongs rather to ancient than to modern literature. It is in the style, not of Davila and Clarendon, but of Herodotus and Tacitus. The classical histories may almost be called romances founded in fact. The relation is, no doubt, in all its principal points, strictly true. But the numerous little incidents which heighten the interest, the words, the gestures, the looks, are evidently furnished by the imagination of the author. The fashion of later times is different. A more exact narrative is given by the writer.

It may be doubted whether more exact notions are conveyed to the reader. The best portraits are perhaps those in which there is a slight mixture of caricature, and we are not certain that the best histories are not those in which a little of the exaggeration of fictitious narrative is judiciously employed. Something is lost in accuracy, but much is gained in effect. The fainter lines are neglected, but the great characteristic features are imprinted on the mind forever.

The *History* terminates with the death of Lorenzo de' Medici. Machiavelli had, it seems, intended to continue his narrative to a later period. But his death prevented the execution of his design, and the melancholy task of recording the desolation and shame of Italy devolved on Guicciardini.

Machiavelli lived long enough to see the commencement of the last struggle for Florentine liberty. Soon after his death monarchy was finally established, not such a monarchy as that of which Cosimo had laid the foundations deep in the institutions and feelings of his countrymen, and which Lorenzo had embellished with the trophies of every science and every art, but a loathsome tyranny, proud and mean, cruel and feeble, bigoted and lascivious. The character of Machiavelli was hateful to the new masters of Italy, and those parts of his theory which were in strict accordance with their own daily practice afforded a pretext for blackening his memory. His works were misrepresented by the learned, misconstrued by the ignorant, censured by the Church, abused with all the rancour of simulated virtue by the tools of a base government and the priests of a baser superstition. The name of the man whose genius had illuminated all the dark places of policy, and to whose patriotic wisdom an oppressed people had owed their last chance of emancipation and revenge, passed into a proverb of infamy. For more than 200 years his bones lay undistinguished. At length, an English nobleman paid the last honours to the greatest statesman of Florence. In the church of Santa Croce a monument was erected to his memory, which is contemplated with reverence by all who can distinguish the virtues of a great mind through the corruptions of a degenerate age, and which will be approached with still deeper homage when the object to which his public life was devoted shall be attained, when the foreign yoke shall be broken, when a second Procida shall avenge the wrongs of Naples, when a happier Rienzi shall restore the good estate of Rome, when the streets of Florence and Bologna shall again resound with their ancient war cry, "*Popolo; popolo; muoiano i tiranni!*"[6]

THE ART OF POWER

NOTES

[1] "Nick Machiavel had ne'er a trick, / Tho' he gave his name to our old Nick" – from Canto I of Part III (1678) of *Hudibras* by Samuel Butler.

[2] "The ladies and the knights, the toils and sports to which love and courtesy stirred our desire there where all hearts have grown so evil." From Dante, "Purgatorio," Canto 14, ll. 109–111.

[3] Jonathan Wild was the most famous criminal in 18th-century London, possibly the whole of Britain.

[4] In the original essay Macaulay had here some critical remarks on the poetry of Machiavelli (though he spared the comedies), but he omitted them on republication, as has been done here.

[5] Machiavelli's little novel of *Belphegor* is pleasantly conceived, and pleasantly told. But the extravagance of the satire in some measure injures its effect. He was unhappily married; and his wish to avenge his own cause, and that of his brethren in misfortune, carried him beyond even the licence of fiction. Jonson seems to have combined some hints taken from this tale, with others from Boccaccio, in the plot of *The Devil is an Ass*, a play which, though not the most highly finished of his compositions, is perhaps that which exhibits the strongest proofs of genius.

[6] "The people! The people! Death to the tyrants!" From Machiavelli's *History of Florence*, Book III.

"THE QUESTION OF MACHIAVELLI"

BY ISAIAH BERLIN

AN EDITED VERSION OF AN ESSAY THAT APPEARED ORIGINALLY IN
THE NEW YORK REVIEW OF BOOKS, 4 NOVEMBER 1971

Part I

There is something surprising about the sheer number of interpretations of Machiavelli's political opinions. There exist, even now, over a score of leading theories of how to interpret *The Prince* and the *Discourses* – apart from a cloud of subsidiary views and glosses. The bibliography of this is vast and growing faster than ever. While there may exist no more than the normal extent of disagreement about the meaning of particular terms or theses contained in these works, there is a startling degree of divergence about the central view, the basic political attitude of Machiavelli.

This phenomenon is easier to understand in the case of other thinkers whose opinions have continued to puzzle or agitate mankind – Plato, for example, or Rousseau or Hegel or Marx. But then it might be said that Plato wrote in a world and in a language that we cannot be sure we understand; that Rousseau, Hegel, Marx were prolific theorists and that their works are scarcely models of clarity or consistency. But *The Prince* is a short book: its style is usually described as being singularly lucid, succinct, and pungent – a model of clear Renaissance prose. The *Discourses* are not, as treatises on politics go, of undue length and they are equally clear and definite. Yet there is no consensus about the significance of either; they have not been absorbed into the texture of traditional political theory; they continue to arouse passionate feelings; *The Prince* has evidently excited the interest and admiration of some of the most formidable men of action of the last four centuries, especially our own, men not normally addicted to reading classical texts.

There is evidently something peculiarly disturbing about what Machiavelli said or implied, something that has caused profound and lasting uneasiness. Modern scholars have pointed out certain real or apparent inconsistencies between the (for the most part) republican sentiment of the *Discourses* (and the *Histories*) and the advice to absolute rulers in *The Prince*; indeed there is a difference of tone between the two treatises, as well as chronological puzzles: this raises problems about Machiavelli's character, motives, and convictions which for three hundred years and more have formed a rich field of investigation and speculation for literary and linguistic scholars, psychologists and historians.

But it is not this that has shocked Western feeling. Nor can it be only Machiavelli's "realism" or his advocacy of brutal or unscrupulous or ruthless politics that has so deeply upset so many later thinkers, and driven some of them to explain or explain away his advocacy of force and fraud. The fact that the wicked are seen to flourish or that immoral courses appear to pay has never been very remote from the consciousness of mankind. The Bible, Herodotus, Thucydides, Plato, Aristotle – to take only some of the fundamental works of Western culture – the characters of Jacob or Joshua, Samuel's advice to Saul, Thucydides' Melian dialogue or his account of at least one ferocious but rescinded Athenian resolution, the philosophies of Thrasymachus and Callicles, Aristotle's advice to tyrants in the *Politics*, Carneades' speeches to the Roman Senate as described by Cicero, Augustine's view of the secular State from one vantage point, and Marsilio's from another – all these had cast enough light on political realities to shock the credulous out of uncritical idealism.

The explanation can scarcely lie in Machiavelli's tough-mindedness alone, even though he did perhaps dot the i's and cross the t's more sharply than anyone before him. Even if the initial outcry – the reactions of, say, Pole or Gentillet – is to be so explained, this does not account for the reactions of those acquainted with the views of Hobbes or Spinoza or Hegel or the Jacobins and their heirs. Something else is surely needed to account both for the continuing horror and for the differences among the commentators. The two phenomena may not be unconnected. To indicate the nature of the latter phenomenon let me cite only the best known rival interpretations of Machiavelli's political views produced since the sixteenth century.

According to Alberico Gentili and Garrett Mattingly, the author of *The Prince* wrote a satire, for he certainly cannot literally have meant what he said. For Spinoza, Rousseau, Ugo Foscolo, Luigi Ricci (who introduces *The Prince* to the readers of The World's Classics) it is a cautionary tale; for whatever else he was, Machiavelli was a passionate patriot, a democrat, a believer in liberty, and *The Prince* must have been intended (Spinoza is particularly clear on this) to warn men of what tyrants could be and do, the better to resist them. Perhaps the author could not write openly with two rival powers – those of the Church and of the Medici – eyeing him with equal (and not unjustified) suspicion. *The Prince* is therefore a satire (though no work seems to me to read less like one).

For A.H. Gilbert it is anything but this – it is a typical piece of its period, a mirror for princes, a genre exercise common enough in the Renaissance and before (and after) it, with very obvious borrowings and "echoes"; more gifted than most of these, and certainly more hard-boiled (and influential); but not so very different in style, content, or intention.

Giuseppe Prezzolini and Hiram Haydn, more plausibly, regard it as an anti-Christian piece (in this following Fichte and others) and see it as an attack on the Church and all her principles, a defence of the pagan view of life. Giuseppe Toffanin, however, thinks Machiavelli was a Christian, though a somewhat peculiar one, a view from which Roberto Ridolfi, his most distinguished living biographer, and Leslie Walker (in his English edition of the *Discourses*) do not wholly dissent. Alderisio, indeed, regards him as a sincere Catholic, although he does not go quite so far as Richelieu's agent, Canon Louis Machon, in his

Apology for Machiavelli, or the anonymous nineteenth-century compiler of *Religious Maxims Faithfully Extracted from the Works of Niccolò Machiavelli* (referred to by Ridolfi in the last chapter of his biography).

For Benedetto Croce and all the many scholars who have followed him Machiavelli is an anguished humanist, and one who, so far from seeking to soften the impression made by the crimes that he describes, laments the vices of men which make such wicked courses politically unavoidable – a moralist who "occasionally experiences moral nausea" in contemplating a world in which political ends can be achieved only by means that are morally evil, and thereby the man who divorced the province of politics from that of ethics. But for the Swiss scholars Walder, Kaegi and von Muralt he is a peace-loving humanist, who believed in order, stability, pleasure in life, in the disciplining of the aggressive elements of our nature into the kind of civilised harmony that he found in its finest form among the well-armed Swiss democracies of his own time. [See *The Prince* chapter 12.]

For the neo-Stoic Justus Lipsius and a century later for Algarotti (in 1759) and Alfieri (in 1796) he was a passionate patriot, who saw in Cesare Borgia the man who, if he had lived, might have liberated Italy from the barbarous French and Spaniards and Austrians who were trampling on her and had reduced her to misery and poverty, decadence and chaos. Garrett Mattingly could not credit this because it was obvious to him, and he did not doubt that it must have been no less obvious to Machiavelli, that Cesare was incompetent, a mountebank, a squalid failure; while Eric Vögelin seems to suggest that it is not Cesare, but (of all men) Tamerlane who was hovering before Machiavelli's fancy-laden gaze.

For Cassirer, Renaudet, Olschki, and Keith Hancock, Machiavelli is a cold technician, ethically and politically uncommitted, an objective analyst of politics, a morally neutral scientist, who (Karl Schmid tells us) anticipated Galileo in applying inductive methods to social and historical material, and had no moral interest in the use made of his technical discoveries – equally ready to place them at the disposal of liberators and despots, good men and scoundrels. Renaudet describes his method as "purely positivist", Cassirer, as concerned with "political statics". For Federico Chabod, though, he is not coldly calculating at all, but passionate to the point of unrealism. Ridolfi, too, speaks of *il grande appassionato* and de Caprariis thinks him positively visionary.

For Herder he is, above all, a marvellous mirror of his age, a man sensitive to the contours of his time, who faithfully described what others did not admit or recognise, an inexhaustible mine of acute contemporary observation; and this is accepted by Ranke and Macaulay, Burd, and, in our day, Gennaro Sasso. For Fichte he is a man of deep insight into the real historical (or super-historical) forces that mould men and transform their morality – in particular, a man who rejected Christian principles for those of reason, political unity, and centralisation. For Hegel he is the man of genius who saw the need for uniting a chaotic collection of small and feeble principalities into a coherent whole; his specific nostrums may excite disgust, but they are accidents due to the conditions of their own time, now long past; yet, however obsolete his precepts, he understood something move important – the demands of his own age – that the hour had struck for the birth of the modern, centralised, political State, for the formation of which he "established the truly necessary fundamental principles".

The thesis that Machiavelli was above all an Italian and a patriot, speaking principally to his own generation, and if not solely to Florentines, at any rate only to Italians, and must be judged solely, or at least mainly, in terms of his historical context is a position common to Herder and Hegel, Macaulay and Burd, de Sanctis and Oreste Tommasini.[1] Yet for Herbert Butterfield and Raffaello Ramat he suffers from an equal lack of scientific and historical sense. Obsessed by classical authors, his gaze is on an imaginary past; he deduces his political maxims in an unhistorical and a priori manner from dogmatic axioms (according to Lauri Huovinen) – a method that was already becoming obsolete at the time in which he was writing; in this

THE ART OF POWER

respect his slavish imitation of antiquity is judged to be inferior to the historical sense and sagacious judgement of his friend Guicciardini (so much for the discovery in him of inklings of modern scientific method).

For Bacon (as for Spinoza, and later for Lassalle) he is above all the supreme realist and avoider of Utopian fantasies. Boccalini is shocked by him, but cannot deny the accuracy or importance of his observations; so is Meinecke, for whom he is the father of *Staatsräson*, with which he plunged a dagger into the body politic of the West, inflicting a wound which only Hegel would know how to heal (this is Meinecke's optimistic verdict in the 1920s, apparently withdrawn after the Second World War).

For König he is not a tough-minded realist or cynic at all, but an aesthete seeking to escape from the chaotic and squalid world of the decadent Italy of his time into a dream of pure art, a man not interested in practice who painted an ideal political landscape; much (if I understand this view correctly) as Piero della Francesca painted an ideal city, *The Prince* is to be read as an idyll in the best neo-classical, neo-pastoral, Renaissance style (yet De Sanctis in the second volume of his *History of Italian Literature* denies it a place in the humanist tradition on account of Machiavelli's hostility to imaginative visions).

For Renzo Sereno it is a fantasy indeed, but of a bitterly frustrated man, and its dedication is the "desperate plea" of a victim of "Fortune's great and steady malice". A psychoanalytic interpretation of one queer episode in Machiavelli's life is offered in support of his thesis.

For Macaulay Machiavelli is a political pragmatist and a patriot who cared most of all for the independence of Florence, and acclaimed any form of rule that would ensure it. Marx calls the *History of Florence* a "masterpiece", and Engels (in the *Dialectics of Nature*) speaks of Machiavelli as one of the "giants" of the Enlightenment, a man free from *petit-bourgeois* outlook. Soviet criticism is more ambivalent.[2]

For the restorers of the short-lived Florentine republic he was evidently nothing but a venal and treacherous toady, anxious to serve any master, who had unsuccessfully tried to flatter the Medici in the hope of gaining their favor. George Sabine (in his well-known textbook) views him as an anti-metaphysical empiricist, a Hume or Popper before his time, free from obscurantist, theological, and metaphysical preconceptions. For Antonio Gramsci he is above all a revolutionary innovator who directs his shafts against the obsolescent feudal aristocracy and papacy and their mercenaries; his *Prince* is a myth which signifies the dictatorship of new, progressive forces: ultimately the coming role of the masses and of the need for the emergence of new politically realistic leaders – *The Prince* is "an anthropomorphic symbol" of the hegemony of the "collective will".

Like Jakob Burckhardt and Friedrich Meinecke, C. J. Friedrich and Charles Singleton maintain that he has a developed conception of the State as a work of art; the great men who have founded or maintain human associations are conceived as analogous to artists whose aim is beauty, and whose essential qualification is understanding of their material – they are moulders of men, as sculptors are moulders of marble or clay. Politics, in this view, leaves the realm of ethics, and approaches that of aesthetics. Singleton argues that Machiavelli's originality consists in his view of political action as a form of what Aristotle called "making" – the goal of which is a non-moral artefact, an object of beauty or use external to man (in this case a particular arrangement of human affairs) – and not of "doing" (where Aristotle and Aquinas had placed it), the goal of which is internal and moral, not the creation of an object, but a particular kind – the right way – of living or being.

This position is not distant from that of Villari, Croce and others, inasmuch as it ascribes to Machiavelli the divorce of politics from ethics. Singleton transfers Machiavelli's conception of politics to the region of art, which is conceived as being amoral. Croce gives it an independent status of its own: of politics for politics' sake.

But the commonest view of him, at least as a political thinker, is still that of most Elizabethans, dramatists and scholars alike, for whom he is a man inspired by the Devil to lead good men to their doom, the great subverter, the teacher of evil, *le docteur de la scélératesse*, the inspirer of St Bartholomew's Eve, the original of Iago. This is the "murderous Machiavel" of the famous 400-odd references in Elizabethan literature. His name adds a new ingredient to the more ancient figure of Old Nick. For the Jesuits he is "the devil's partner in crime", "a dishonourable writer and an unbeliever", and *The Prince* is, in Bertrand Russell's words, "a handbook for gangsters" (compare with this Mussolini's description of it as a "*vade mecum* for statesmen", a view tacitly shared, perhaps, by other heads of State). This is the view common to Protestants and Catholics, Gentillet and François Hotman, Cardinal Pole, Bodin and Frederick the Great, followed by the authors of all the many anti-Machiavels, the latest of whom are Jacques Maritain and Leo Strauss.

There is prima facie something strange about so violent a disparity of judgements. What other thinker has presented so many facets to the students of his ideas? What other writer – and he not even a recognised philosopher – has caused his readers to disagree about his purposes so deeply and so widely? Yet, I must repeat, Machiavelli does not write obscurely; nearly all his interpreters praise him for his terse, dry, clear prose.

What is it that has proved so arresting to so many?

Part II

Machiavelli, we are often told, was not concerned with morals. The most influential of all modern interpretations – that of Benedetto Croce, followed to some extent by Chabod, Russo, and others – is that Machiavelli, in E.W. Cochrane's words:

"did not deny the validity of Christian morality, and did not pretend that a crime required by political necessity was any the less a crime. Rather he discovered...that this morality simply did not hold in political affairs, and that any policy based on the assumption that it did, would end in disaster. His factual objective description of contemporary practices is a sign not of cynicism or detachment but of anguish."

This account, it seems to me, contains two basic misinterpretations. The first is that the clash is one between "Christian morality" and "political necessity". The implication is that there is an incompatibility between, on the one hand, morality – the region of ultimate values sought after for their own sakes, values recognition of which alone enables us to speak of "crimes" or morally to justify and condemn anything; and on the other, politics – the art of adapting means to ends, the region of technical skills, of what Kant was to call "hypothetical imperatives", which take the form "If you want to achieve x, do y" (for example, betray a friend, kill an innocent man) without necessarily asking whether x is itself intrinsically desirable or not. This is the heart of the divorce of politics from ethics which Croce and many others attribute to Machiavelli. But this seems to me to rest on a mistake.

If ethics is confined to, let us say, Stoic or Christian or Kantian, or even some types of utilitarian ethics, where the source and criterion of value are the word of God, or eternal reason, or some inner sense or knowledge of good and evil, of right and wrong, voices which speak directly to the individual consciousness with absolute authority, this might have been tenable. But there exists an equally time-honored ethics, that of the Greek *polis*, of which Aristotle provided the clearest exposition. Since men are beings made by nature to live in communities, their communal purposes are the ultimate values from which the rest are derived, or with which their ends as individuals are identified. Politics – the art of living in a *polis* – is not an activity that can be dispensed with by those who prefer private life: it is not like seafaring or sculpture which those who do not wish to do so need not undertake. Political conduct is intrinsic to being a human being at a certain stage of civilisation, and what it demands is intrinsic to living a successful human life.

Ethics so conceived – the code of conduct of, or the ideal to be pursued by, the individual – cannot be known save by understanding the purpose and character of his *polis*; still less be capable of being divorced from it, even in thought. This is the kind of pre-Christian morality which Machiavelli takes for granted. "It is well-known", says Benedetto Croce, "that Machiavelli discovered the necessity and autonomy of politics, which is beyond moral good and evil, which has its own laws against which it is useless to rebel, which cannot be exorcised and made to vanish by holy water." Beyond good and evil in some non-Aristotelian, religious, or liberal-Kantian sense; but not beyond the good and evil of those communities, ancient or modern, whose sacred values are social through and through. The arts of colonisation or of mass murder (let us say) may also have their "own laws against which it is useless to rebel" for those who wish to practise them successfully. But if or when these laws collide with those of morality, it is possible, and indeed morally imperative, to abandon such activities.

But if Aristotle and Machiavelli are right about what men are (and should be – and Machiavelli's ideal is, particularly in the *Discourses*, drawn in vivid colours), political activity is intrinsic to human nature, and while individuals here and there may opt out, the mass of mankind cannot do so; and its communal life determines the moral duties of its members. Hence in opposing the "laws of politics" to "good and evil" Machiavelli is not contrasting two "autonomous" spheres of acting – the "political" and the "moral": he is contrasting his own "political" ethics with another ethical conception which governs the lives of persons who are of no interest to him. He is indeed rejecting one morality – the Christian – but not in favour of something that is not a morality at all but a game of skill, an activity called political, which is not concerned with ultimate human ends and is therefore not ethical at all.

He is indeed rejecting Christian ethics, but in favor of another system, another moral universe – the world of Pericles or of Scipio, or even of the Duke Valentino, a society geared to ends just as ultimate as the Christian faith, a society in which men fight and are ready to die for (public) ends which they pursue for their own sakes. They are choosing not a realm of means (called politics) as opposed to a realm of ends (called morals), but opt for a rival (Roman or classical) morality, an alternative realm of ends. In other, words the conflict is between two moralities, Christian and pagan (or as some wish to call it, aesthetic), not between autonomous realms of morals and politics.

Nor is this a mere question of nomenclature, unless politics is conceived as being concerned not (as it usually is) with means, skills, methods, technique, "know-how" (whether or not governed by unbreakable rules of its own), but with an independent kingdom of ends of its own, sought for their own sake, a substitute for ethics. When Machiavelli said (in a letter to Francesco Vettori) that he loved his native city more than his own soul, he revealed his basic moral beliefs – a position with which Croce does not credit him.

The second thesis in this connection which seems to me mistaken is the idea that Machiavelli viewed the crimes of his society with anguish. (Chabod in his excellent study, unlike Croce and some Croceans, does not insist on this.) This entails that he accepts the dire necessities of the *raison d'état* with reluctance, because he sees no alternative. But there is no evidence for this: there is no trace of agony in his political works, any more than in his plays or letters.

The pagan world that Machiavelli prefers is built on recognition of the need for systematic guile and force by rulers, and he seems to think it natural and not at all exceptional or morally agonising that they should employ these weapons wherever they are needed. Nor does he seem to think exceptional the distinction he draws between the rulers and the ruled. The subjects or citizens must be Romans too: they do not need the *virtù* of the rulers, but if they also cheat, Machiavelli's maxims will not work; they must be poor, militarised, honest, and obedient; if they lead Christian lives, they will accept too uncomplainingly the rule of mere bullies and scoundrels. No sound republic can be built of such materials as these. Theseus and Romulus, Moses and Cyrus did not preach humility or a view of this world as but a temporary resting place.

But it is the first misinterpretation that goes deepest, that which represents Machiavelli as caring little or nothing for moral issues. This is surely not borne out by his own language. Anyone whose thought revolves round central concepts such as the good and the bad, the corrupt and the pure, has an ethical scale in mind in terms of which he gives moral praise and blame. Machiavelli's values are not Christian, but they are moral values.

On this crucial point Hans Baron's criticism of the Croce-Russo thesis seems to me correct. Against the view that for Machiavelli politics were beyond moral criticism, Baron cites some of the passionately patriotic, republican and libertarian passages in the *Discourses* in which the (moral) qualities of the citizens of a republic are favourably compared with those of the subjects of a despotic prince. The last chapter of *The Prince* is scarcely the work of a detached, morally neutral observer, or of a self-absorbed man, preoccupied with his own inner personal problems, who looks on public life "with anguish" as the graveyard of moral principles. Like Aristotle's or Cicero's, Machiavelli's morality was social and not individual: but it was a morality no less than theirs, not an amoral region, beyond good or evil.

It does not, of course, follow that he was not often fascinated by the techniques of political life as such. The advice given equally to conspirators and their enemies, the professional appraisal of the methods of Oliverotto or Sforza or Baglioni spring from typical humanist curiosity, the search for an applied science of politics, fascination by knowledge for its own sake, whatever the implications. But the moral ideal, that of the citizen of the Roman Republic, is never far away. Political skills are valued solely as means – for their effectiveness in re-creating conditions in which sick men recover their health and can flourish. And this is precisely what Aristotle would have called the moral end proper to man.

This leaves still with us the thorny problem of the relation of *The Prince* to the *Discourses*. But whatever the disparities, the central strain which runs through both is one and the same. The vision – the dream – typical of many writers who see themselves as tough-minded realists – of the strong, united, effective, morally regenerated, splendid and victorious *patria*, whether it is saved by the *virtù* of one man or many – remains central and constant. Political judgements, attitudes towards individuals or states, to *fortuna*, and *necessità*, evaluation of methods, degree of optimism, the fundamental mood – these vary between one work and another, perhaps within the same exposition. But the basic values, the ultimate end –Machiavelli's beatific vision – does not vary.

His vision is social and political. Hence the traditional view of him as simply a specialist in how to get the better of others, a vulgar cynic who says that Sunday-school precepts are all very well, but in a world full of evil men you too must lie, kill and so on if you are to get somewhere, is incorrect. The philosophy summarised by "Eat or be eaten, beat or be beaten" – the kind of worldly wisdom to be found in, say, Lappo Mazzei or Giovanni Morelli, with whom he has been compared – is not what is central in him. Machiavelli is not specially concerned with the opportunism of ambitious individuals; the ideal before his eyes is a shining vision of Florence or of Italy. In this respect he is a typically impassioned humanist of the Renaissance, save that his ideal is not artistic or cultural but political, unless the state – or regenerated Italy – is considered, in Burckhardt's sense, as an artistic goal. This is very different from mere advocacy of tough-mindedness as such, or of a realism irrespective of its goal.

Machiavelli's values, I should like to repeat, are not instrumental but moral and ultimate, and he calls for great sacrifices in their name. For them he rejects the rival scale – the Christian principles of *ozio* and meekness – not, indeed, as being defective in itself, but as inapplicable to the conditions of real life; and real life for him means not merely (as is sometimes alleged) life as it was lived around him in Italy – the crimes, hypocrisies, brutalities, follies of Florence, Rome, Venice, Milan. This is not the touchstone of reality. His purpose is not to leave unchanged or to reproduce this kind of life, but to lift it to a new plane, to rescue Italy from squalor and slavery, to restore her to health and sanity.

The moral ideal for which he thinks no sacrifice too great – the welfare of the *patria* – is for him the highest form of social existence attainable by man; but attainable, not unattainable; not a world outside the limits of human capacity, given human beings as we know them, that is, creatures compounded out of those emotional, intellectual, and physical properties of which history and observation provide examples. He asks for men improved but not transfigured, not superhuman; not for a world of ideal beings unknown on this earth, who, even if they could be created, could not be called human.

If you object to the political methods recommended because they seem to you morally detestable, if you refuse to embark upon them because they are, to use Ritter's word, "*erschreckend*", too frightening, Machiavelli has no answer, no argument. In that case you are perfectly entitled to lead a morally good life, be a private citizen (or a monk), seek some corner of your own. But, in that event, you must not make yourself responsible for the lives of others or expect good fortune; in a material sense you must expect to be ignored or destroyed.

In other words you can opt out of the public world, but in that case he has nothing to say to you, for it is to the public world and to the men in it that he addresses himself. This is expressed most clearly in his notorious advice to the victor who has to hold down a conquered province. He advises a clean sweep: new governors, new titles, new powers, and new men; he should:

"make the rich poor, the poor rich, as David did when he became king…who 'heaped riches on the needy and dismissed the wealthy empty-handed'. Besides this, he should build new cities, overthrow those already built, change the inhabitants from one place to another; and in short he should leave nothing in that province untouched, and make sure that no rank or position or office or wealth is held by anyone who does not acknowledge it as from you". [3]

He should take Philip of Macedon as his model, who "by proceeding in that manner became…master of all Greece". Now Philip's historian informs us – Machiavelli goes on to say – that he transferred the inhabitants from one province to another "as shepherds move their flocks" from one place to another. Doubtless, Machiavelli continues:

"These methods are cruel, and enemies to all government not merely Christian but human, and any man ought to avoid them and prefer to live a private life rather than to be a king who brings such ruin on men. Notwithstanding, a ruler who does not wish to take that first good way of lawful government, if he wishes to maintain himself, must enter upon this evil one. But men take certain middle ways that are very injurious; indeed, they are unable to be altogether good or altogether bad."[4]

This is plain enough. There are two worlds, that of personal morality and that of public organisation. There are two ethical codes, both ultimate; not two "autonomous" regions, one of "ethics", another of "politics", but two (for him) exhaustive alternatives between two conflicting systems of value. If a man chooses the "first, humane course", he must presumably give up all hope of Athens and Rome, of a noble and glorious society in which human beings can thrive and grow strong, proud, wise and productive. Indeed, he must abandon all hope of a tolerable life on earth: for men cannot live outside society; they will not survive collectively if they are led by men who (like Soderini) are influenced by the first, "private" morality; they will not be able to realise their minimal goals as men; they will end in a state of moral, not merely political, degradation. But if a man chooses, as Machiavelli himself has done, the second course, then he must suppress his private qualms, if he has any, for it is certain that those who are too squeamish during the remaking of a society, or even during its pursuit and maintenance of its power and glory, will go to the wall. Whoever has chosen to make an omelette cannot do so without breaking eggs.

Machiavelli is sometimes accused of too much relish at the prospect of breaking eggs – almost for its own sake. This is unjust. He thinks these ruthless methods are necessary – necessary as means to provide good results, good in terms not of a Christian, but of a secular, humanistic, naturalistic morality. His most shocking examples show this. The most famous, perhaps, is that of Giovanpaolo Baglioni, who caught Julius II during one of his campaigns, and let him escape, when in Machiavelli's view he might have destroyed him and his cardinals and thereby committed a crime "the greatness of which would have transcended every infamy, every peril that could have resulted from it".

Like Frederick the Great (who called Machiavelli "the enemy of mankind" and followed his advice),[5] Machiavelli is, in effect, saying "*Le vin est tiré: il faut le boire*". Once you embark on a plan for the transformation of a society you must carry it through no matter at what cost: to fumble, to retreat, to be overcome by scruples is to betray your chosen cause. To be a physician is to be a professional, ready to burn, to cauterize, to amputate; if that is what the disease requires, then to stop halfway because of personal qualms, or some rule unrelated to your art and its technique, is a sign of muddle and weakness, and will always give you the worst of both worlds. And there are at least two worlds: each of them has much, indeed everything, to be said for it; but they are two and not one. One must learn to choose between them and, having chosen, not look back.

There is more than one world, and more than one set of virtues: confusion between them is disastrous. One of the chief illusions caused by ignoring this is the Platonic-Hebraic-Christian view that virtuous rulers create virtuous men. This, according to Machiavelli, is not true. Generosity is a virtue, but not in princes. A generous prince will ruin the citizens by taxing them too heavily, a mean prince (and Machiavelli does not say that meanness is a good quality in private men) will save the purses of the citizens and so add to public welfare. A kind ruler – and kindness is a virtue – may let intriguers and stronger characters dominate him, and so cause chaos and corruption.

Other writers of "Mirrors for Princes" are also rich in such maxims, but they do not draw the implications. Machiavelli's use of such generalisations is not theirs; he is not moralising at large, but illustrating a specific thesis: that the nature of men dictates a public morality that is different from, and may come into collision with, the virtues of men who profess to believe in, and try to act by, Christian precepts. These may not be wholly unrealisable in quiet times, in private life, but they lead to ruin outside this. The analogy between a state and people and an individual is a fallacy: "The state and people are governed in a different way from an individual." "It is not the well-being of individuals that makes cities great, but of the community."

One may disagree with this. One may argue that the greatness, glory, and wealth of a state are hollow ideals, or detestable, if the citizens are oppressed and treated as mere means to the grandeur of the whole. Like Christian thinkers, or like Constant and the liberals, or like Sismondi and the theorists of the welfare state, one may prefer a state in which citizens are prosperous even though the public treasury is poor, in which government is neither centralised nor omnipotent, nor, perhaps, sovereign at all, but the citizens enjoy a wide degree of individual freedom; one may contrast this favorably with the great authoritarian concentrations of power built by Alexander or Frederick the Great or Napoleon, or the great autocrats of the twentieth century.

If so, one is simply contradicting Machiavelli's thesis: he sees no merit in such loose political textures. They cannot last. Men cannot long survive in such conditions. He is convinced that states that have lost the appetite for power are doomed to decadence and are likely to be destroyed by their more vigorous and better armed neighbours; and Vico and modern "realistic" thinkers have echoed this.

Part III

Machiavelli is possessed by a clear, intense, narrow vision of a society in which human talents can be made to contribute to a powerful and splendid whole. He prefers republican rule in which the interests of the rulers do not conflict with those of the ruled. But (as Macaulay perceived) he prefers a well-governed principate to a decadent republic, and the qualities he admires and thinks capable of being welded into – indeed, indispensable to – a durable society are not different in *The Prince* and the *Discourses*: energy, boldness, practical skill, imagination, vitality, self-discipline, shrewdness, public spirit, good fortune, *antiqua virtus*, *virtù* – firmness in adversity, strength of character, as celebrated by Xenophon or Livy. All his more shocking maxims – those responsible for the "murd'rous Machiavel" of the Elizabethan stage – are descriptions of methods of realising this single end: the classical, humanistic, and patriotic vision that dominates him.

Let me cite the best known of his most notoriously wicked pieces of advice to princes. One must employ terrorism or kindness, as the case dictates. Severity is usually more effective, but humanity, in some situations, brings better fruit. You may excite fear but not hatred, for hatred will destroy you in the end. It is best to keep men poor and on a permanent war footing, for this will be an antidote to the two great enemies of obedience – ambition and boredom – and the ruled will then feel in constant need of great men to lead them (the twentieth century offers us only too much evidence for this sharp insight). Competition – divisions between classes – in a society is desirable, for it generates energy and ambition in the right degree.

Religion must be promoted even though it may be false, provided it is of a kind that preserves social solidarity and promotes manly virtues, as Christianity has historically failed to do. When you confer benefits (he says, following Aristotle), do so yourself; but if dirty work is to be done, let others do it, for then they, not the prince, will be blamed and the prince can gain favour by duly cutting off their heads: for men prefer vengeance and security to liberty. Do what you must do in any case, but try to represent it as a special favour to the people. If you must commit a crime do not advertise it beforehand, since otherwise your enemies may destroy you before you destroy them. If your action must be drastic, do it in one fell swoop, not in agonising stages. Do not be surrounded by over-powerful servants – victorious generals are best got rid of, otherwise they may get rid of you.

You may be violent and use your power to overawe, but you must not break your own laws, for that destroys confidence and disintegrates the social texture. Men should either be caressed or annihilated; appeasement and neutralism are always fatal. Excellent plans without arms are not enough or else Florence would still be a republic. Rulers must live in the constant expectation of war. Success creates more devotion than an amiable character; remember the fate of Pertinax, Savonarola, Soderini. Severus was unscrupulous and cruel, Ferdinand of

Spain is treacherous and crafty: but by practising the arts of both the lion and the fox they escaped both snares and wolves. Men will be false to you unless you compel them to be true by creating circumstances in which falsehood will not pay. And so on.

These examples are typical of "the devil's partner". Now and then doubts assail our author: he wonders whether a man high-minded enough to labour to create a state admirable by Roman standards will be tough enough to use the violent and wicked means prescribed; and, conversely, whether a sufficiently ruthless and brutal man will be disinterested enough to compass the public good which alone justifies the evil means. Yet Moses and Theseus, Romulus and Cyrus combined these properties.[6] What has been once can be again: the implication is optimistic.

All these maxims have one property in common: they are designed to create or resurrect or maintain an order that will satisfy what the author conceives as men's most permanent interests. Machiavelli's values may be erroneous, dangerous, odious; but he is in earnest. He is not cynical. The end is always the same: a state conceived after the analogy of Periclean Athens, or Sparta, but above all the Roman Republic. Such an end, for which men naturally crave (of this he thinks that history and observation provide conclusive evidence), "excuses" any means. In judging means, look only to the end: if the state goes under, all is lost. Hence the famous paragraph in the forty-first chapter of the third book of the *Discourses* where he says:

"when the very safety of the country depends upon the resolution to be taken, no considerations of justice or injustice, humanity or cruelty, not of glory or of infamy, should be allowed to prevail. But putting all other considerations aside, the only question should be 'What course will save the life and liberty of the country?'"

The French have reasoned thus, and the "majesty of their king and the greatness of France" have come from it. Romulus could not have founded Rome without killing Remus. Brutus would not have preserved the republic if he did not kill his sons. Moses and Theseus, Romulus, Cyrus, and the liberators of Athens had to destroy in order to build. Such conduct, so far from being condemned, is held up to admiration by the classical historians and the Bible. Machiavelli is their admirer and faithful spokesman.

What is there, then, about his words, about his tone, which has caused such tremours among his readers? Not, indeed, in his own lifetime – there was a delayed reaction of some quarter of a century. But after that it is one of continuous and mounting horror. Fichte, Hegel, Treitschke "reinterpreted" his doctrines and assimilated them to their own views. But the sense of horror was not thereby greatly mitigated. It is evident that the effect of the shock that he administered was not a temporary one: it has lasted almost to our own day.

Leaving aside the historical problem of why there was no immediate contemporary criticism, let us consider the continuous discomfort caused to its readers during the four centuries that have passed since *The Prince* was placed upon the Index. The great originality, the tragic implications of Machiavelli's theses seem to me to reside in their relation to a Christian civilisation. It was all very well to live by the light of pagan ideals in pagan times; but to preach paganism more than a thousand years after the triumph of Christianity was to do so after the loss of innocence – and to be forcing men to make a conscious choice. The choice is painful because it is a choice between two entire worlds. Men have lived in both, and fought and died to preserve them against each other. Machiavelli has opted for one of them, and he is prepared to commit crimes for its sake.

In killing, deceiving, betraying, Machiavelli's princes and republicans are doing evil things not condonable in terms of common morality. It is Machiavelli's great merit that he does not deny this. Marsilio, Hobbes, Spinoza, and, in their own fashion, Hegel and Marx did try to deny it. So did many a defender of the *raison d'état*, Imperialist and Populist, Catholic and Protestant. These thinkers argue for a single moral system, and seek to show that the morality which justifies, and indeed demands, such deeds is continuous with, and a more rational form of, the confused ethical beliefs of the uninstructed morality which forbids them absolutely.

From the vantage-point of the great social objectives in the name of which these (prima facie wicked) acts are to be performed, they will be seen (so the argument goes) as no longer wicked, but as rational – demanded by the very nature of things, by the common good, or man's true ends, or the dialectic of history – condemned only by those who cannot or will not see a large enough segment of the logical or theological or metaphysical or historical pattern; misjudged, denounced only by the spiritually blind or short-sighted. At worst, these "crimes" are discords demanded by the larger harmony, and therefore, to those who hear this harmony, no longer discordant.

Machiavelli is not a defender of any such abstract theory. It does not occur to him to employ such casuistry. He is transparently honest and clear. In choosing the life of a statesman, or even the life of a citizen with enough civic sense to want his state to be as successful and splendid as possible, a man commits himself to rejection of Christian behaviour.[7] It may be that Christians are right about the well-being of the individual soul, taken outside the social or political context. But the well-being of the state is not the same as the well-being of the individual – "they cannot be governed in the same way". You have made your choice: the only crimes are weakness, cowardice, stupidity which may cause you to draw back in midstream and fail.

Compromise with current morality leads to bungling, which is always despicable, and when practised by statesmen involves men in ruin. The end "excuses" the means, however horrible these may be in terms of even pagan ethics, if it is (in terms of the ideal of Thucydides or Polybius, Cicero or Livy) lofty enough. Brutus was right to kill his children: he saved Rome. Soderini did not have the stomach to perpetrate such deeds, and ruined Florence. Savonarola, who had sound ideas about austerity and moral strength and corruption, perished because he did not realise that an unarmed prophet will always go to the gallows.

If one can produce the right result by using the devotion and affection of men, let this be done by all means. There is no value in causing suffering as such. But if one cannot, then

Moses, Romulus, Theseus, Cyrus are the exemplars, and fear must be employed. There is no sinister satanism in Machiavelli, nothing of Dostoevsky's great sinner, pursuing evil for evil's sake. To Dostoevsky's famous question "Is everything permitted?" Machiavelli, who for Dostoevsky would surely have been an atheist, answers, "Yes, if the end – that is, the pursuit of a society's basic interests in a specific situation – cannot be realised in any other way."

This position has not been properly understood by some of those who claim to be not unsympathetic to Machiavelli. Figgis, for example, thinks that he "permanently suspended the *habeas corpus* of the human race", that is to say, that he advocated methods of terrorism because for him the situation was always critical, always desperate, so that he confused ordinary political principles with rules needed, if at all, only in extreme cases.

Others – perhaps the majority of his interpreters – look on him as the originator, or at least a defender, of what later came to be called "*raison d'état*", "*Staatsraison*", "*Ragion di Stato*" – the justification of immoral acts when undertaken on behalf of the state in exceptional circumstances. More than one scholar has pointed out, reasonably enough, that the notion that desperate cases require desperate remedies – that "necessity knows no law" – is to be found not only in antiquity but equally in Aquinas and Dante and other medieval writers long before Bellarmino or Machiavelli.

These parallels seem to me to rest on a deep but characteristic misunderstanding of Machiavelli's thesis. He is not saying that while in normal situations current morality – that is, the Christian or semi-Christian code of ethics – should prevail, yet abnormal conditions can occur, in which the entire social structure in which alone this code can function becomes jeopardised, and that in emergencies of this kind acts that are usually regarded as wicked and rightly forbidden are justified.

This is the position of, among others, those who think that all morality ultimately rests on the existence of certain institutions – say, Roman Catholics who regard the existence of the Church and the Papacy as indispensable to Christianity, or nationalists who see in the political power of a nation the sole source of spiritual life. Such persons maintain that extreme and "frightful" measures needed for protecting the state or the Church or the national culture in moments of acute crisis may be justified, since the ruin of these institutions may fatally damage the indispensable framework of all other values. This is a doctrine in terms of which both Catholics and Protestants, both conservatives and communists have defended enormities which freeze the blood of ordinary men.

But this is not Machiavelli's position. For the defenders of the *raison d'état*, the sole justification of these measures is that they are exceptional – that they are needed to preserve a system the purpose of which is precisely to preclude the need for such odious measures, so that the sole justification of such steps is that they will end the situations that render them necessary. But for Machiavelli these measures are, in a sense, themselves quite normal. No doubt they are called for only by extreme need; yet political life tends to generate a good many such needs, of varying degrees of "extremity"; hence Baglioni, who shied from the logical consequences of his own policies, was clearly unfit to rule.

The notion of *raison d'état* entails a conflict of values which may be agonising to morally good and sensitive men. For Machiavelli there is no conflict. Public life has its own morality, to which Christian principles (or any absolute personal values) tend to be a gratuitous obstacle. This life has its own standards: it does not require perpetual terror, but it approves, or at least permits, the use of force where it is needed to promote the ends of political society.

Sheldon Wolin[8] seems to me right in insisting that Machiavelli believes in a permanent "economy of violence" – the need for a consistent reserve of force always in the background to keep things going in such a way that the virtues admired by him, and by the classical thinkers to whom he appeals, can be protected and allowed to flower. Men brought up within a community in which such force, or its possibility, is used rightly will live the happy lives of Greeks or Romans during their finest hours. They will be characterised by vitality, genius, variety, pride, power, success (Machiavelli scarcely ever speaks of arts or sciences); but it will not, in any clear sense, be a Christian commonwealth. The moral conflict which this situation raises will trouble only those who are not prepared to abandon either course: those who assume that the two incompatible lives are, in fact, reconcilable.

But to Machiavelli the claims of the official morality are scarcely worth discussing: they are not translatable into social practice. "If men were good..." but he feels sure that they can never be improved beyond the point at which power considerations are relevant. If morals relate to human conduct, and men are by nature social, Christian morality cannot be a guide for normal social existence. It remained for someone to state this. Machiavelli did so.

One is obliged to choose: and in choosing one form of life, give up the other. That is the central point. If Machiavelli is right, if it is in principle (or in fact: the frontier seems dim) impossible to be morally good and do one's duty as this was conceived by common European, and especially Christian, ethics, and at the same time build Sparta or Periclean Athens or the Rome of the Republic or even of the Antonines, then a conclusion of the first importance follows: that the belief that the correct, objectively valid solution to the question of how men should live can in principle be discovered is itself, in principle, not true. This was a truly *erschreckend* proposition. Let me try to put it in its proper context.

One of the deepest assumptions of Western political thought is the doctrine, scarcely questioned during its long ascendancy, that there exists some single principle that not only regulates the course of the sun and the stars, but prescribes their proper behaviour to all animate creatures. Animals and subrational beings of all kinds follow it by instinct; higher beings attain to consciousness of it, and are free to abandon it, but only to their doom. This doctrine in one version or another has dominated European thought since Plato; it has appeared in many forms, and has generated many similes and allegories. At its centre is

the vision of an impersonal Nature or Reason or cosmic purpose, or of a divine Creator whose power has endowed all things
and creatures each with a specific function; these functions are
elements in a single harmonious whole, and are intelligible in
terms of it alone.

This was often expressed by images taken from architecture: of a great edifice of which each part fits uniquely in the
total structure; or from the human body as an all-embracing
organic whole; or from the life of society as a great hierarchy,
with God as the *ens realissimum* at the summit of two parallel
systems – the feudal order and the natural order – stretching downward from Him, and reaching upward to Him, obedient to His will. Or it is seen as the Great Chain of Being, the
Platonic-Christian analogue of the world-tree Ygdrasil, which
links time and space and all that they contain. Or it has been
represented by an analogy drawn from music, as an orchestra
in which each instrument or group of instruments has its own
tune to play in the infinitely rich polyphonic score. When, after
the seventeenth century, harmonic metaphors replaced polyphonic images, the instruments were no longer conceived as
playing specific melodies, but as producing sounds which, although they might not be wholly intelligible to any given group
of players (and even sound discordant or superfluous if taken in
isolation), yet contributed to the total pattern perceptible only
from a loftier standpoint.

The idea of the world and of human society as a single intelligible structure is at the root of all the many various versions
of Natural Law – the mathematical harmonies of the Pythago-
reans, the logical ladder of Platonic Forms, the genetic-logical
pattern of Aristotle, the divine *Logos* of the Stoics and the Christian churches and of their secularised offshoots. The advance of
the natural sciences generated more empirically conceived versions of this image as well as anthropomorphic similes: of Dame
Nature as an adjuster of conflicting tendencies (as in Hume or
Adam Smith), of Mistress Nature as the teacher of the best way
to happiness (as in the works of some French Encyclopaedists),
of Nature as embodied in the actual customs or habits of organ-

ised social wholes; biological, aesthetic, psychological similes have reflected the dominant ideas of an age.

This unifying monistic pattern is at the very heart of traditional rationalism, religious and atheistic, metaphysical and scientific, transcendental and naturalistic, which has been characteristic of Western civilisation. It is this rock, upon which Western beliefs and lives had been founded, that Machiavelli seems, in effect, to have split open. So great a reversal cannot, of course, be due to the acts of a single individual. It could scarcely have taken place in a stable social and moral order; many besides him, ancient Skeptics, medieval nominalists and secularists, Renaissance humanists, doubtless supplied their share of the dynamite. The purpose of this paper is to suggest that it was Machiavelli who lit the fatal fuse.

If to ask what are the ends of life is to ask a real question, it must be capable of being correctly answered. To claim rationality in matters of conduct was to claim that correct and final solutions to such questions can in principle be found. When such solutions were discussed in earlier periods, it was normally assumed that the perfect society could be conceived, at least in outline; for otherwise what standard could one use to condemn existing arrangements as imperfect? It might not be realisable here, below. Men were too ignorant or too weak or too vicious to create it. Or it was said (by some materialistic thinkers in the centuries following *The Prince*) that it was technical means that were lacking, that no one had yet discovered methods of overcoming the material obstacles to the golden age; that we were not technologically or educationally or morally sufficiently advanced. But it was never said that there was something incoherent in the very notion itself.

Plato and the Stoics, the Hebrew prophets and Christian medieval thinkers, and the writers of utopias from More onwards had a vision of what it was that men fell short of; they claimed, as it were, to be able to measure the gap between the reality and the ideal. But if Machiavelli is right, this entire tradition — the central current of Western thought — is fallacious. For if his position is valid then it is impossible to construct even the notion of such a perfect society, for there exist at least two sets of virtues – let us call them the Christian and the pagan – which are not merely in practice, but in principle, incompatible.

If men practise Christian humility, they cannot also be inspired by the burning ambitions of the great classical founders of cultures and religions; if their gaze is centred upon the world beyond – if their ideas are infected by even lip-service to such an outlook – they will not be likely to give all that they have to an attempt to build a perfect city. If suffering and sacrifice and martyrdom are not always evil and inescapable necessities, but may be of supreme value in themselves, then the glorious victories over fortune, which go to the bold, the impetuous, and the young, might neither be won nor thought worth winning. If spiritual goods alone are worth striving for, then of how much value is the study of *necessità* – of the laws that govern nature and human lives – by the manipulation of which men might accomplish unheard-of things in the arts and the sciences and the organisation of social lives?

To abandon the pursuit of secular goals may lead to disintegration and a new barbarism; but even if this is so, is this the worst that could happen? Whatever the differences between Plato and Aristotle, or of either of these thinkers from the Sophists or Epicureans or the other Greek schools of the fourth and later centuries, they and their disciples, the European rationalists and empiricists of the modern age, were agreed that the study of reality by minds undeluded by appearances could reveal the correct ends to be pursued by men – that which would make men free and happy, strong and rational.

Some thought that there was a single end for all men in all circumstances, or different ends for men of different kinds or in dissimilar historical environments. Objectivists and universalists were opposed by relativists and subjectivists, metaphysicians by empiricists, theists by atheists. There was profound disagreement about moral issues; but what none of these thinkers, not even the Skeptics, had suggested was that there might exist ends – ends in themselves in terms of which alone everything else was justified – which were equally ultimate, but incompatible with one another, that there might exist no single universal overarching standard that would enable a man to choose rationally between them.

This was indeed a profoundly upsetting conclusion. It entailed that if men wished to live and act consistently, and understand what goals they were pursuing, they were obliged to examine their moral values. What if they found that they were compelled to make a choice between two incommensurable systems? To choose as they did without the aid of an infallible measuring rod which certified one form of life as being superior to all others and which could be used to demonstrate this to the satisfaction of all rational men? Is it, perhaps, this awful truth, implicit in Machiavelli's exposition, that has upset the moral consciousness of men, and has haunted their minds so permanently and obsessively ever since?

Machiavelli did not himself propound it. There was no problem and no agony for him; he shows no trace of scepticism or relativism; he chose his side, and took little interest in the values that this choice ignored or flouted. The conflict between his scale of values and that of conventional morality clearly did not (*pace* Croce and the other defenders of the "anguished humanist" interpretation) seem to worry Machiavelli himself. It upset only those who came after him, and were not prepared, on the one hand, to abandon their own moral values (Christian or humanist) together with the entire way of thought and action of which these were a part; nor, on the other, to deny the validity of, at any rate, much of Machiavelli's analysis of the political facts, and the (largely pagan) values and outlook that went with it, embodied in the social structure which he painted so brilliantly and convincingly.

Whenever a thinker, however distant from us in time or culture, still stirs passion, enthusiasm, or indignation, any kind of intense debate, it is generally the case that he has propounded a thesis that upsets some deeply established *idée reçue*, a thesis that those who wish to cling to the old conviction nevertheless find it hard or impossible to dismiss or refute. This is the case with Plato, Hobbes, Rousseau, Marx. I should like to suggest that it is Machiavelli's juxtaposition of the two outlooks – the two incompatible moral worlds, as it were – in the minds of his readers, and the collision and acute discomfort that follow that, over the years, has been responsible for the desperate efforts to interpret his doctrines away, to represent him as a cynical and therefore ultimately shallow defender of power politics; or as a diabolist; or as a patriot prescribing for particularly desperate situations which seldom arise; or as a mere time server; or as an embittered political failure; or as a mere mouthpiece of truths we have always known but did not like to utter; or again as the enlightened translator of universally accepted ancient social principles into empirical terms; or as a crypto-republican satirist (a descendant of Juvenal, a forerunner of Orwell); or as a cold scientist, a mere political technologist free from moral implications; or as a typical Renaissance publicist practising a now obsolete genre; or in any of the numerous other roles that have been and are still being cast for him.

Machiavelli may have possessed some of these attributes, but concentration on one or other of them as constituting his essential, "true" character seems to me to stem from reluctance to face and, still more, discuss the uncomfortable truth that Machiavelli had, unintentionally, almost casually, uncovered: namely, that not all ultimate values are necessarily compatible with one another – that there might be a conceptual (what used to be called "philosophical"), and not merely a material, obstacle to the notion of the single ultimate solution which, if it were only realised, would establish the perfect society.

Part IV

Yet if no such solution can, even in principle, be formulated, then all political and, indeed, moral problems are thereby transformed. This is not a division of politics from ethics. It is the uncovering of the possibility of more than one system of values, with no criterion common to the systems whereby a rational choice can be made between them. This is not the rejection of Christianity for paganism (although Machiavelli clearly prefers the latter), nor of paganism for Christianity (which, at least in its historical form, he thought incompatible with the basic needs of normal men), but the setting of them side by side with the implicit invitation to men to choose either a good, virtuous private life or a good, successful social existence, but not both.

What has been shown by Machiavelli, who is often (like Nietzsche) congratulated for tearing off hypocritical masks, brutally revealing the truth, and so on, is not that men profess one thing and do another (although no doubt he shows this too) but that when they assume that the two ideals are compatible, or perhaps are even one and the same ideal, and do not allow this assumption to be questioned, they are guilty of bad faith (as the existentialists call it, or of "false consciousness", to use a Marxist formula) which their actual behaviour exhibits. Machiavelli calls the bluff not just of official morality – the hypocrisies of ordinary life – but of one of the foundations of the central Western philosophical tradition, the belief in the ultimate compatibility of all genuine values. His own withers are unwrung. He has made his choice. He seems wholly unworried by, indeed scarcely aware of, parting company with traditional Western morality.

But the question that his writings have dramatised, if not for himself, then for others in the centuries that followed, is this: what reason have we for supposing that justice and mercy, humility and *virtù*, happiness and knowledge, glory and liberty, magnificence and sanctity will always coincide, or indeed be compatible at all? Poetic justice is, after all, so called not because it does, but because it does not, as a rule, occur in the prose of ordinary life, where, *ex hypothesi*, a very different kind of justice operates. "States and people are governed in a different way from an individual." Hence what talk can there be of indestructible rights, either in the medieval or the liberal sense? The wise man must eliminate fantasies from his own head, and should seek to dispel them from the heads of others; or, if they are too resistant, he should at least, as Pareto or Dostoevsky's Grand Inquisitor recommended, exploit them as a means to a viable society.

"The march of world history stands outside virtue, vice and justice", said Hegel. If for the march of history you substitute "a well governed *patria*", and interpret Hegel's notion of virtue as it is understood by Christians or ordinary men, then Machiavelli is one of the earliest proponents of this doctrine. Like all great innovators, he is not without ancestry. But the names of Palmieri and Pontano, and even of Carneades and Sextus Empiricus, have left little mark on European thought.

Croce has rightly insisted that Machiavelli is not detached nor cynical nor irresponsible. His patriotism, his republicanism, his commitment are not in doubt. He suffered for his convictions. He thought continually about Florence and Italy, and of how to save them. Yet it is not his character, nor his plays, his poetry, his histories, his diplomatic or political activities that have gained him his unique fame.[9] Nor can this be due only to his psychological or sociological imagination. His psychology is often excessively primitive. He scarcely seems to allow for the bare possibility of sustained and genuine altruism, he refuses to consider the motives of men who are prepared to fight against enormous odds, who ignore *necessità* and are prepared to lose their lives in a hopeless cause.

His distrust of unworldly attitudes, absolute principles divorced from empirical observation, is fanatically strong — almost romantic in its violence; the vision of the great prince playing upon human beings like an instrument intoxicates him. He assumes that different societies must always be at war with each other, since they have conflicting purposes. He sees history as one endless process of cutthroat competition, in which the only goal that rational men can have is to succeed in the eyes of their contemporaries and of posterity. He is good at bringing fantasies down to earth, but he assumes, as Mill was to complain about Bentham, that this is enough. He allows too little to the ideal impulses of men. He has no historical sense and little sense of economics. He has no inkling of the technological progress that is about to transform political and social life, and in particular the art of war. He does not understand how either individuals, communities, or cultures develop and transform themselves. Like Hobbes, he assumes that the argument or motive for self-preservation automatically outweighs all others.

He tells men above all not to be fools: to follow a principle when this may involve you in ruin is absurd, at least if judged by worldly standards; other standards he mentions respectfully, but takes no interest in them: those who adopt them are not likely to create anything that will perpetuate their name. His Romans are no more real than the stylised figures in his brilliant comedies. His human beings have so little inner life or capacity for cooperation or social solidarity that, as in the case of Hobbes's not dissimilar creatures, it is difficult to see how they could develop enough reciprocal confidence to create a lasting social whole, even under the perpetual shadow of carefully regulated violence.

Few would deny that Machiavelli's writings, more particularly *The Prince*, have scandalised mankind more deeply and continuously than any other political treatise. The reason for this, let me say again, is not the discovery that politics is the play of power – that political relationships between and within independent communities involve the use of force and fraud, and are unrelated to the principles professed by the players. That knowledge is as old as conscious thought about politics – certainly as old as Thucydides and Plato. Nor is it merely caused by the examples that he offers of success in acquiring or holding power – the descriptions of the massacre at Sinigaglia or the behaviour of Agathocles or Oliverotto da Fermo are no more or less horrifying than similar stories in Tacitus or Guicciardini. The proposition that crime can pay is nothing new in Western historiography.

Nor is it merely his recommendation of ruthless measures that so upsets his readers. Aristotle had long ago allowed that exceptional situations might arise, that principles and rules could not be rigidly applied to all situations; the advice to rulers in *The Politics* is tough-minded enough. Cicero is aware that critical situations demand exceptional measures; *ratio publicae utilitatis, ratio status* were familiar in the thought of the Middle Ages. "Necessity is not subject to law" is a Thomist sentiment;

Pierre d'Auvergne says much the same. Harrington said this in the following century, and Hume applauded him.

These opinions were not thought original by these, or perhaps any, thinkers. Machiavelli did not originate nor did he make much use of the notion of *raison d'état*. He stressed will, boldness, address, at the expense of the rules laid down by the calm *ragione*, to which his colleagues in the *Pratiche Fiorentine*, and perhaps the Oricellari Gardens, may have appealed. So did Leon Battista Alberti when he declared that *fortuna* crushes only the weak and propertyless; so did contemporary poets; so, too, in his own fashion, did Pico della Mirandola in his great apostrophe to the powers of man the creator, who, unlike the angels, can transform himself into any shape – the ardent image that lies at the heart of European humanism in the North as well as the Mediterranean.

Far more original, as has often been noted, is Machiavelli's divorce of political behaviour as a field of study from the theological world picture in terms of which this topic was discussed before him (even by Marsilio) and after him. Yet it is not his secularism, however audacious in his own day, that could have disturbed the contemporaries of Voltaire or Bentham or their successors. What shocked them is something different.

Machiavelli's cardinal achievement is his uncovering of an insoluble dilemma, the planting of a permanent question mark in the path of posterity. It stems from his *de facto* recognition that ends equally ultimate, equally sacred, may contradict each other, that entire systems of value may come into collision without possibility of rational arbitration, and that not merely in exceptional circumstances, as a result of abnormality or accident or error – the clash of Antigone and Creon or in the story of Tristan – but (this was surely new) as part of the normal human situation.

For those who look on such collisions as rare, exceptional, and disastrous, the choice to be made is necessarily an agonising experience for which, as a rational being, one cannot prepare (since no rules apply). But for Machiavelli, at least in *The Prince*, the *Discourses*, *Mandragola*, there is no agony. One chooses as one chooses because one knows what one wants, and is ready to pay the price. One chooses classical civilisation rather than the Theban desert, Rome and not Jerusalem, whatever the priests may say, because such is one's nature, and – he is no existentialist or romantic individualist *avant la parole* – because it is that of men in general, at all times, everywhere. If others prefer solitude or martyrdom, he shrugs his shoulders. Such men are not for him. He has nothing to say to them, nothing to argue with them about. All that matters to him and those who agree with him is that such men be not allowed to meddle with politics or education or any of the cardinal factors in human life; their outlook unfits them for such tasks.

I do not mean that Machiavelli explicitly asserts that there is a pluralism or even a dualism of values between which conscious choices must be made. But this follows from the contrasts he draws between the conduct he admires and that which he condemns. He seems to take for granted the obvious superiority of classical civic virtue and brushes aside Christian values, as well as conventional morality, with a disparaging or patronising sentence or two, or smooth words about the misinterpretation of Christianity.[10] This worries or infuriates those who disagree with him the more because it goes against their convictions without seeming to be aware of doing so – and recommends wicked courses as obviously the most sensible, something that only fools or visionaries will reject.

If what Machiavelli believed is true, this undermines one major assumption of Western thought: namely, that somewhere in the past or the future, in this world or the next, in the church or the laboratory, in the speculations of the metaphysician or the findings of the social scientist or in the uncorrupted heart of the simple good man, there is to be found the final solution of the question of how men should live. If this is false (and if more than one equally valid answer to the question can be returned, then it is false) the idea of the sole true, objective, universal human ideal crumbles. The very search for it becomes not merely utopian in practice, but conceptually incoherent.

One can surely see how this might seem unfaceable to men, believers or atheists, empiricist or apriorists, brought up on the opposite assumption. Nothing could well be more upsetting to those brought up in a monistic religious or, at any rate, moral, social, or political system than a breach in it. This is the dagger of which Meinecke speaks, with which Machiavelli inflicted the wound that has never healed; even though Felix Gilbert is right in thinking that he did not bear the scars of it himself. For he remained a monist, albeit a pagan one.

Machiavelli was doubtless guilty of much confusion and exaggeration. He confused the proposition that ultimate ideals may be incompatible with the very different proposition that the more conventional human ideals – founded on ideas of Natural Law, brotherly love, and human goodness – were unrealisable and that those who acted on the opposite assumption were fools, and at times dangerous ones; and he attributed this dubious proposition to antiquity and believed that it was verified by history. The first of these assertions strikes at the root of all doctrines committed to the possibility of attaining, or at least formulating, final solutions; the second is empirical, commonplace, and not self-evident. The two propositions are not, in any case, identical or logically connected.

Moreover he exaggerated wildly: the idealised types of the Periclean Greek or the Roman of the old Republic may be irreconcilable with the ideal citizen of a Christian commonwealth (supposing such were conceivable), but in practice – above all in history, to which our author went for illustrations if not for evidence – pure types seldom obtain: mixtures and compounds and compromises and forms of communal life that do not fit into easy classifications, but which neither Christians nor liberal humanists nor Machiavelli would be compelled by their beliefs to reject, can be conceived without too much intellectual difficulty. Still, to attack and inflict lasting damage on a central assumption of an entire civilisation is an achievement of the first order.

Machiavelli does not affirm this dualism. He merely takes for granted the superiority of Roman *antiqua virtus* (which may be maddening to those who do not) over the Christian life as taught by the Church. He utters a few casual words about what Christianity might have become, but does not expect it to change its actual character. There he leaves the matter. Anyone who believes in Christian morality regards the Christian Commonwealth as its embodiment, but at the same time largely accepts the validity of Machiavelli's political and psychological analysis and does not reject the secular heritage of Rome – a man in this predicament is faced with a dilemma which, if Machiavelli is right, is not merely unsolved, but insoluble. This is the Gordian knot which, according to Vanini and Leibniz, the author of *The Prince* had tied, a knot which can only be cut, not untied. Hence the efforts to dilute his doctrines, or interpret them in such a way as to remove their sting.

After Machiavelli, doubt is liable to infect all monistic constructions. The sense of certainty that there is somewhere a hidden treasure – the final solution to our ills – and that some path must lead to it (for, in principle, it must be discoverable); or else, to alter the image, the conviction that the fragments constituted by our beliefs and habits are all pieces of a jigsaw puzzle, which (since there is an a priori guarantee for this) can, in principle, be solved; so that it is only because of lack of skill or stupidity or bad fortune that we have not so far succeeded in discovering the solution whereby all interests will be brought into harmony – this fundamental belief of Western political thought has been severely shaken. Surely in an age that looks for certainties, this is sufficient to account for the unending efforts, more numerous today than ever, to explain *The Prince* and the *Discourses*, or to explain them away?

This is the negative implication. There is also one that is positive, and might have surprised and perhaps displeased Machiavelli. So long as only one ideal is the true goal, it will always seem to men that no means can be too difficult, no price too high, to do whatever is required to realise the ultimate goal. Such certainty is one of the great justifications of fanaticism, compulsion, persecution. But if not all values are compatible with one another, and choices must be made for no better reason than that each value is what it is, and we choose it for what it is, and not because it can be shown on some single scale to be higher than another. If we choose forms of life because we believe in them, because we take them for granted, or, upon examination, find that we are morally unprepared to live in any other way (although others choose differently); if rationality and calculation can be applied only to means or subordinate ends, but never to ultimate ends; then a picture emerges different from that constructed round the ancient principle that there is only one good for men.

If there is only one solution to the puzzle, then the only problems are first how to find it, then how to realise it, and finally how to convert others to the solution by persuasion or by force. But if this is not so (Machiavelli contrasts two ways of life, but there could be, and, save for fanatical monists, there obviously are, more than two), then the path is open to empiricism, pluralism, toleration, compromise. Toleration is historically the product of the realisation of the irreconcilability of equally dogmatic faiths, and the practical improbability of complete victory of one over the other. Those who wished to survive realised that they had to tolerate error. They gradually came to see merits in diversity, and so became sceptical about definitive solutions in human affairs.

But it is one thing to accept something in practice, another to justify it rationally. Machiavelli's "scandalous" writings begin the latter process. This was a major turning point, and its intellectual consequences, wholly unintended by its originator, were, by a fortunate irony of history (which some call its dialectic), the basis of the very liberalism that Machiavelli would surely have condemned as feeble and characterless, lacking in single-minded pursuit of power, in splendour, in organisation, in *virtù*, in power to discipline unruly men against huge odds into one energetic whole. Yet he is, in spite of himself, one of the makers of pluralism, and of its – to him – perilous acceptance of toleration.

By breaking the original unity he helped to cause men to become aware of the necessity of making agonising choices between incompatible alternatives, incompatible in practice or, worse still, for logical reasons, in public and private life (for the two could not, it became obvious, be genuinely kept distinct). His achievement is of the first order, if only because the dilemma has never given men peace since it came to light (it remains unsolved, but we have learned to live with it). Men had, no doubt, in practice, often enough experienced the conflict that Machiavelli made explicit. He converted its expression from a paradox into something approaching a commonplace.

The sword of which Meinecke spoke has not lost its edge: the wound has not healed. To know the worst is not always to be liberated from its consequences; nevertheless it is preferable to ignorance. It is this painful truth that Machiavelli forced on our attention, not by formulating it explicitly, but perhaps the more effectively by relegating much uncriticised traditional morality to the realm of utopia. This is what, at any rate, I should like to suggest. Where more than twenty interpretations hold the field, the addition of one more cannot be deemed an impertinence. At worst it will be no more than yet another attempt to solve the problem, now more than four centuries old, of which Croce at the end of his long life spoke as *"una questione che forse non si chiuderà mai: la questione de Machiavelli"*.[11]

NOTES

[1] Ernst Cassirer makes the valid and relevant point that to value – or justify – Machiavelli's opinions solely as a mirror of their times is one thing; to maintain that he was himself consciously addressing only his own countrymen, and, if Burd is to be believed, not even all of them, is a very different one, and entails a false view of him and the civilisation to which he belonged. The Renaissance did not view itself in historical perspective. Machiavelli was looking for – and thought that he had found – timeless, universal truths about social behavior. It is no service either to him or to the truth to deny or ignore the unhistorical assumptions which he shared with all his contemporaries and predecessors. The praise lavished upon him by the German historical school from Herder onwards, including the Marxist Antonio Gramsci, for the gifts in which they saw his strength – his realistic sense of his own times, his insight into the rapidly changing social and political conditions of Italy and Europe in his time, the collapse of feudalism, the rise of the national State, the altering power relationships within the Italian principalities and the lik – might have been galling to a man who believed he had discovered eternal verities. He may, like his countryman Columbus, have mistaken the nature of his own achievement. If the historical school (including the Marxists) is right, Machiavelli did not do, and could not have done, what he set out to do. But nothing is gained by supposing he did

not set out to do it; and plenty of witnesses from his day to ours would deny Herder's assertion, and maintain that Machiavelli's goal – the discovery of the permanent principles of a political science – was anything but Utopian; and that he came nearer than most to attaining it.

[2] "The only extended treatment of Machiavelli by a prominent Bolshevik intellectual known to me is in Kamenev's short-lived introduction to the Russian translation of *The Prince* (Moscow, 1934), reprinted in English as "Preface to Machiavelli", *New Left Review* No 15 (May–June 1962), 39–42. This unswervingly follows the full historicist-sociological approach criticised by Cassirer. Machiavelli is described as an active publicist, preoccupied by the "mechanism of the struggles for power" within and between the Italian principalities, a sociologist who gave a masterly analysis of the "sociological" jungle that preceded the formation of a "powerful, national, essentially bourgeois" Italian State. His almost "dialectical" grasp of the realities of power, and freedom from metaphysical and theological fantasies, establish him as a worthy forerunner of Marx, Engels, Lenin and Stalin. These opinions were brought up at Kamenev's trial and pilloried by Vyshinsky, the prosecutor. See on this Chimen Abramsky, "Kamenev's Last Essay", *New Left Review*, No 15 (May–June 1962), pp. 34–38.

[3] *Discourses* i p. 26.

[4] *Discourses* i p. 26.

[5] It is still not clear how much of this Frederick owed to his mentor Voltaire.

[6] H. L. Trevor-Roper has drawn my attention to the irony of the fact that the heroes of this supreme realist are all, wholly or in part, mythical.

[7] At the risk of exhausting the patience of the reader, I must repeat that this is a conflict not of pagan statecraft with Christian morals, but of pagan morals (indissolubly connected with social life and inconceivable without it) with Christian ethics which, whatever its implication for politics, can be stated independently of it, as, e.g., Aristotle's or Hegel's ethics cannot.

[8] Sheldon S. Wolin, *Politics and Vision*, Little, Brown: London, 1960, pp. 220–224.

[9] The moral of his best comedy, *Mandragola*, seems to me close to that of the political tracts: that the ethical doctrines professed by the characters are wholly at variance with what they do to attain their various ends. Virtually every one of them in the end obtains what he wants; if Callimaco had resisted temptation, or the lady he seduces had been smitten with remorse, or Fra Timoteo attempted to practice the maxims of the Fathers and the Schoolmen with which he liberally seasons his speeches, this could not have occurred. But all turns out for the best, though not from the point of view of accepted morality. If the play castigates hypocrisy and stupidity, the standpoint is not that of virtue but of candid hedonism. The notion that Callimaco is a kind of Prince in private life, successful in creating and maintaining his own world by the correct use of guile and fraud, the exercise of *virtù* and a bold challenge to *fortuna*, appears highly plausible. For this, see Henry Paolucci (trans.) *Mandragola*, Library of Liberal Arts: New York, 1957.

[10] For example, in the passages from the *Discourses* cited above, or as when he says, "I believe that the greatest good that can be done, and the most pleasing to God, is that which is done to one's country." My thanks are due to Professor Myron Gilmore for this reference to *The Discourse on Reforming Florence*. This sentiment is by no means unique in Machiavelli's works: but, leaving aside his wish to flatter

Leo X, or the liability of all authors to fall into the clichés of their own time, are we to suppose that Machiavelli means us to think that when Philip of Macedon transplanted populations in a manner that (unavoidable as it is said to have been) caused even Machiavelli a qualm, what Philip did, provided it was good for Macedon, was pleasing to God and, *per contra*, that Giovanpaolo Baglioni's failure to kill the Pope and the Curia were displeasing to Him? Such a notion of the deity is, to say the least, remote from that of the New Testament. Are the needs of the patria automatically identical with the will of the Almighty? Are those who permit themselves to doubt this in danger of heresy? Machiavelli may at times have been represented as too Machiavellian; but to suppose that he believed that the claims of God and of Caesar were perfectly reconcilable reduces his central thesis to absurdity. Yet of course this does not prove that he lacked all Christian sentiment: the *Esortanzione alla pentitenza* composed in the last year of his life (if it is genuine and not a later forgery) may well be wholly sincere, as Ridolfi and Alderisio believe; Capponi may have exaggerated the extent to which he "drove religion from his heart", even though "it was not wholly extinct in his thought". The point is that there is scarcely any trace of such *états d'âme* in his political writings with which alone we are concerned. There is an excellent discussion of that by Giuseppe Prezzolini in his article, "The Christian Roots of Machiavelli's Moral Pessimism," pp. 26–27 (*Review of National Literatures*, Vol. I, No. I, New York, 1970) in which this attitude is traced to Augustine, and Croce's thesis is, by implication, controverted.

[11] A question that perhaps will never be resolved: the question of Machiavelli.

CHRONOLOGY

1469 – Niccolò Machiavelli born (May 3)

1494 – Republic declared in Florence

1498 – Machiavelli selected Second Chancellor of the Republic (June); appointed secretary to the Ten of War (July)

1499 – Machiavelli acts as legate on an embassy to Catherine Sforza (Countess of Forli)

1500 – Machiavelli acts as legate on an embassy to France

1502 – Piero Soderini chosen *gonfaloniere* of Florence; Machiavelli is the accredited agent of the Florentine Republic to Cesare Borgia in Rome

1507 – Machiavelli acts as legate on an embassy to Emperor Maximilian

1512 – Florence surrenders to Spanish troops; Medici family returns (September); Machiavelli sacked as Second Chancellor (November)

1513 – Machiavelli arrested and imprisoned (February); begins to compose *The Prince* (finished early 1514?)

1514 – Machiavelli begins writing the *Discourses on the Ten Books of Titus Livy* (finished in 1519?)

1516 – Ferdinand V of Castile (II of Aragon), king of Sicily and Naples, dies

1519 – Maximilian I, Holy Roman Emperor, dies

1521 – Machiavelli's *The Art of War* published

1526 – Machiavelli completes the *History of Florence* and presents it to Pope Clement VII

1527 – Rome sacked and the Medici again overthrown; Machiavelli dies (June 21)

1531 – Machiavelli's *Discourses on the Ten Books of Titus Livy* published

1532 – *The Prince* published by Machiavelli's son

1559 – Machiavelli's collected works are placed on the Index of Prohibited Books by the Sacred Congregation of the Roman Inquisition (of the Roman Catholic Church)

1640 – *The Prince* appears in an English translation by Edward Dacre

PERSONALITIES

Alexander VI, Pope (1431–1503). Born Rodrigo Borgia. He came to Italy from Spain just after 1450 and rode his uncle's ecclesiastical success (he became Pope Calixtus III) to his own ascension to office in 1492. He fathered numerous children, whom he favoured, including Cesare Borgia.

Borgia, Cesare (1475–1507). Using the support of his father, Pope Alexander VI, Cesare first received religious preferment and then sought a secular career. He was made the Duke of Valentinois in 1498 by French king Louis XII. Borgia devoted his career to military and political conquest in Italy thereafter, but with the death of his father his power waned and he was eventually exiled to Spain, where he died.

Charles VIII, king of France (1470–1498). Invaded Italy in 1494 in order to establish his family claim to the Kingdom of Naples. The invasion sparked the retreat of the Medici from Florence and the creation of the Florentine Republic.

Clement VII, Pope (1478–1453). Born Giulio de'Medici, nephew of Lorenzo de'Medici (the Magnificent), he was consecrated archbishop of Florence by his cousin, Pope Leo X. Giulio ruled Florence following the death in 1519 of Lorenzo de'Medici, duke of Urbino, until he was selected pope in 1523.

d'Este, Alfonso I (1476–1534). Duke of Ferrara and husband of Lucrezia Borgia, the daughter of Pope Alexander VI. Alfonso d'Este succeeded in maintaining and extending his sway despite the political and military opposition of the Medici popes.

Julius II, Pope (1443–1513). Born Giuliano della Rovere, he was the nephew of Pope Sixtus IV, who appointed Giuliano a cardinal. Elected pope in 1503, he almost immediately commenced elaborate diplomatic and military manouevres to gain political hegemony over the Papal States, which had asserted autonomy from Rome or had come under the sway of external states, such as Venice. Initially an ally of France, he eventually concluded that French influence in Italy had become too great and entered into an agreement with Spain.

Leo X, Pope (1475–1521). Born Giovanni de'Medici, the second son of Lorenzo de'Medici (the Magnificent). He was made cardinal in 1492, but the French invasion in 1494 and subsequent creation of the Florentine Republic forced him to live abroad for many years. He succeeded Pope Julius II in 1513 and soon became the object of a poisoning attack plotted by a group of cardinals, which he survived. He was active in the early stages of opposition to Martin Luther's reforming movement in Germany.

Louis XII, king of France (1462–1515). Duke of Orleans and king from 1498, he joined Charles VIII in the 1494 invasion of Italy and remained in the northern part of the country for several years thereafter. Louis laid dynastic claim to the Duchy of Milan with an invasion in 1499. He remained a prominent figure in Italian politics through his reign.

Maximillian I, Holy Roman Emperor (1459–1519). Selected as co-king of Germany in 1485, while he father, Emperor Frederick III, was alive. He became sole

German ruler in 1493 and assumed the imperial title in 1508 with the authorization of Pope Julius II.

Medici, Giuliano de' (1479–1516). The third son of Lorenzo de'Medici (the Magnificent). He became the head of the Florentine government after the election of his brother as Pope Leo X. Machiavelli originally intended to dedicate *The Prince* to Giuliano, but he died before a presentation could be arranged.

Medici, Lorenzo de' (1449–1492). Known widely as "The Magnificent," Lorenzo became the undisputed leader of the Medici clan and the leading figure in Florentine politics from 1478 until his death. He was also a leading patron of the arts and of humanist scholarship.

Medici, Lorenzo de', Duke of Urbino (1492–1519). Son of Piero, the eldest son of Lorenzo the Magnificent. Lorenzo the younger became the head of the Florentine government after the death of his brother, Giuliano. Machiavelli dedicated *The Prince* to him.

Petrucci, Pandolfo (1450–1512). Ruler of Siena. He seized power in conjunction with his brother in 1487. An opponent of Cesare Borgia's agenda, Petrucci engaged in extensive military and diplomatic negotiations with France and Florence to limit Borgia's influence, in which goal he ultimately succeeded.

Rucellai, Cosimo (1495–1519). Member of a leading Florentine family, he organized (with his friend Zanobi Buondelmonti) a regular discussion group about Florentine politics held at the Oricellari Gardens, which Machiavelli frequented. Machiavelli's *Discourses on the Ten Books of Titus Livy* is jointly dedicated to Rucellai and Buondelmonti.

Savonarola, Girolamo (1452–1498). Popular Dominican preacher who originally hailed from Ferrara. His sermons contained prophetic visions of remarkable accuracy, as well as extreme denunciations of the immorality of both the laity and the clergy. Following the expulsion of the Medici family from Florence in 1494, Savonarola became the most influential resident of the city and pursued a programme of moral reform in the fledgling Florentine republic – the most spectacular instance of which was the "bonfire of the vanities". His downfall resulted from his principled opposition to clerical misconduct, which attracted the attention and condemnation of Pope Alexander VI. Savonarola's reputation was eroded and he was eventually put to death (publicly hanged and his body then burned) by the republic in 1498 following his excommunication by the pope in 1497.

Sforza, Ludovico, Duke of Milan (1451–1508). Became duke in 1494, after the death of his nephew, for whom he was regent. He urged the French invasion of Italy in 1494 with the hope of extending the territorial reach of Milan. But he authored his own downfall when Milan was attacked in 1499 by France's King Louis XII, who claimed the duchy for himself. Ludovico died a prisoner in a French castle.

Soderini, Piero (1452–1522). Florentine public servant under the Medici and republican governments. Soderini promoted Machivelli's career in the Chancery, especially after becoming *gonfaloniere* or head of government for life, a new office created by the Florentine Great Council in 1502. With the Spanish invasion of Italy in 1512 and the end of the republic in Florence, Soderini escaped to Rome, where he enjoyed the protection of his brother, Cardinal Francesco Soderini.

FURTHER READING

Machiavelli's Writings

Adams, Robert M.(ed. and trans.) *Niccolò Machiavelli, The Prince: A New Translation, Backgrounds, Interpretations*. New York: Norton, 1977.

Banfield, Laura and Mansfield, Harvey C. Jr.(trans.) *Florentine Histories*. Princeton: Princeton University Press, 1988.

Crick, Bernard. (ed.) *Niccolò Machiavelli: The Discourses*. Harmondsworth: Penguin, 1983.

Gilbert, Alan. (ed. and trans.) *Machiavelli: The Chief Works and Others*. (3 vols.) Durham, North Carolina: Duke University Press, 1965.

Sices, David and Atkinson, James B. (ed. and trans.) *The Comedies of Machiavelli*. Hanover: Published for Dartmouth College by University Press of New England, 1985.

Taylor, Quentin P. (ed.) *The Other Machiavelli: Republican Writings by the Author of "The Prince"*. Lanham, Maryland: University Press of American, 1998.

Tusiani, Joseph. (ed. and trans.) *Lust and Liberty: The Poems of Machiavelli*. New York: Obolensky, 1963.

Wood, Neal. (ed.) *Machiavelli: The Art of War*. Indianapolis: Bobbs-Merrill, 1965.

Historical Background

Butters, H.C. *Governors and Government in Early Sixteenth-Century Florence, 1502–1519*. Oxford: Clarendon Press, 1985.

Gilbert, Felix. *Machiavelli and Guicciardini: Politics and History in Sixteenth Century Florence*. New York: Norton, 1984.

Godman, Peter. *From Poliziano to Machiavelli: Florentine Humanism in the High Renaissance*. Princeton: Princeton University Press, 1998.

Hale, J.R. *Florence and the Medici*. London: Phoenix Press, 2001.

Martines, Lauro. *Power and Imagination: City-States in Renaissance Italy*. New York: Vintage Books, 1979.

Rubinstein, Nicolai. *The Government of Florence under the Medici 1434–1494*. (2nd ed.) Oxford: Oxford University Press, 1998.

Skinner, Quentin. *The Foundations of Modern Political Thought. Vol 1: The Renaissance*. Cambridge: Cambridge University Press, 1978.

Viroli, Maurizio. *From Politics to Reason of State*. Cambridge: Cambridge University Press, 1992.

Biography

de Grazia, Sebastian. *Machiavelli in Hell*. New York: Vintage Books, 1994.

Najemy, John M. *Between Friends: Discourses of Desire and Power in the Machiavell-Vettori Letters of 1513–1515*. Princeton: Princeton University Press, 1993.

Villari, Pasquale. *The Life and Times of Niccolò Machiavelli*. (2nd ed., 2 vols., trans. Linda Villari.) New York: Greenwood, 1968.

Viroli, Maurizio. *Niccolò's Smile*. (trans. Antony Shuggar.) New York: Hill and Wang, 2000.

Scholarly Studies

Ascoli, Albert Russell and Kahn, Victoria. (eds.) *Machiavelli and the Discourses*

of Literature. Ithaca, New York: Cornell University Press, 1993.

Bock, Gisela; Skinner, Quentin; and Virloi, Maurizio. (eds.) *Machiavelli and Republicanism*. Cambridge: Cambridge University Press, 1990.

Bondanella, Peter E. *Machiavelli and the Art of Renaissance History*. Detroit: Wayne State University Press, 1973.

Chabod, Federico. *Machiavelli and the Renaissance*. (trans. David Moore.) London: Bowes and Bowes, 1958.

Coyle, Martin. (ed.) *Niccolò Machiavelli's The Prince: New Interdisciplinary Essays*. Manchester: Manchester University Press, 1995.

Falco, Maria J. (ed.) *Feminist Interpretations of Machiavelli*. University Park: Pennsylvania State University Press, 2004.

Fischer, Markus. *Well-Ordered License: On the Unity of Machiavelli's Thought*. Lanham, Maryland: Lexington Books, 2000.

Jensen, De Lamar. (ed.) *Machiavelli: Cynic, Patriot, or Political Scientist?* Lexington, Massachusetts: D.C. Heath, 1960.

Hörnqvist, Mikael. *Machiavelli and Empire*. Cambridge: Cambridge University Press, 2004.

Hulliung, Mark. *Citizen Machiavelli*. Princeton: Princeton University Press, 1983.

Pitkin, Hannah F. *Fortune is a Woman: Gender and Politics in the Thought of Niccolò Machiavelli*. Berkeley: University of California Press, 1984.

Rebhorn, Wayne A. *Lions and Foxes: Machiavelli's Confidence Men*. Ithaca, New York:

Cornell University Press, 1988.

Sasso, Gennaro. *Niccolò Machiavelli: Storia del suo pensiero politico*. (2nd ed.) Bologna: il Mulino, 1980.

Skinner, Quentin. *Machiavelli: A Very Short Introduction*. Oxford: Oxford University Press, 2000.

Strauss, Leo. *Thoughts on Machiavelli*. Chicago: University of Chicago Press, 1978.

Viroli, Maurizio. *Machiavelli*. Oxford: Oxford University Press, 1998.

von Vacano, Diego A. *The Art of Power*. Lanham, Maryland: Lexington Books, 2006.

Later Influence

Anglo, Sydney. *Machiavelli: The First Century*. Oxford: Oxford University Press, 2005.

Fontana, Benedetto. *Hegemony and Power: On the Relation between Gramsci and Machiavelli*. Minneapolis: University of Minnesota Press, 1993.

Kahn, Victoria. *Machiavellian Rhetoric: From the Counterreformation to Milton*. Princeton: Princeton University Press, 1994.

Pocock, John. *The Machiavellian Moment: Florentine Political Thought and the Atlantic Republican Tradition*. Princeton: Princeton University Press, 1975.

Raab, Felix. *The English Face of Machiavelli: A Changing Interpretation 1500–1700*. London: Routledge & Kegan Paul, 1964.

Rahe, Paul. *Republicanism Ancient and Modern: Classical Republicanism and the American Revolution*. Chapel Hill: University of North Carolina Press, 1992.

INDEX

ACKNOWLEDGMENTS

Author acknowledgments

The suggestion for the preparation of this new, illustrated edition of Machiavelli's *The Prince* first came from Christopher Westhorp at Duncan Baird, who has also shepherded the volume through the editorial and production stages of publication. My thanks to Chris for inviting me to participate in this project as well as for his many useful comments on the penultimate version of the introduction. Dr. Karen L. Bollermann of Arizona State University read multiple drafts of the introduction and offered trenchant and meticulous criticism that immensely improved the final product.

Text acknowledgments

The translation in this edition is reproduced from one produced by W.K. Marriott, published by J.M. Dent in 1908, and amended and updated where appropriate by Cary Nederman. New text material is contained in the Introduction, caption illustrations and reference matter. "Machiavelli" by Thomas Babington Macaulay appeared in *The Edinburgh Review* in March 1827. "The Question of Machiavelli" by Isaiah Berlin was published in *The New York Review of Books* on 4 November 1971 and is reproduced here in an edited form with permission of Curtis Brown Group Ltd, London, on behalf of the Isaiah Berlin Literary Trust. © Isaiah Berlin 1971.

PICTURE CREDITS

The publisher would like to thank the following people, museums, and photographic libraries for permission to reproduce their material. Every care has been taken to trace copyright holders. However, if we have omitted anyone we apologize and will, if informed, make corrections to any future edition.

AA The Art Archive, London
BAL The Bridgeman Art Library, London
DO Dagli Orti
Scala Scala Archives, Florence

2 Santi di Tito (1536–1603): Niccolo Machiavelli 1469–1527, detail (Palazzo Vecchio, Florence/BAL); **26** Bonsignori and Danti: Map of Italy from *Sala delle Carte Geografiche*, 1575, fresco (Palazzo Vecchio, Florence/BAL); **28** Giraldi (fl.1445–89), Arms of the House of Este, detail, from *Bible des Chartreux*, vellum (Palazzo Schifanoia, Ferrara/BAL); **30** Bourdichon (1457–1521), *Louis XII (1462–1515) enters Genoa*, vellum (Bibliothèque Nationale, Paris/BAL); **38** Gian Galeazzo Sforza (1468–94) deposed duke of Milan, Italian, late 15c. marble medallion (Musée des Beaux Arts Lyons/DO/AA); **42** Alexander the Great, Roman copy of Greek bust, marble (Pinacoteca Capitolina, Rome/BAL); **44–45** Veronese (1528–1588): *Family of Darius before Alexander*, detail (National Gallery, London); **48** Italian School: Panorama of Florence, detail from the *Carta della Catena*, 1490 (Museo di Firenze Comera, Florence/BAL); **51** Vasari: *Triumph after the war with Pisa*, detail from the ceiling of Salone dei Cinquecento, 1565 (Palazzo Vecchio, Florence/BAL); **52** Dossi (ca.1479-1542): *Alfonso I d'Este (1476–1534)*, detail (Museo Estense, Modena/BAL); **57** L&A della Robbia (1400–82): Savonarola, bronze medallion (Museo Nazionale del Bargello, Florence/BAL); **58** Cola da Roma: Pope Alexander VI and the holders of temporal power, detail from *Madonna dei Raccomandati*, ca.1500 (Museo Diocesano, Orta/DO/AA); **61** Meloni: *Cesare Borgia 1475–1507* (Accademia Carrara, Bergamo/AA);

66–67 Basilica Metropolitano and Palazzo Ducale, Urbino (Lonely Planet Images/Getty Images); 70 Matteo di Giovanni (ca.1430–1495): *Massacre of the Innocents*, detail (Palazzo Pubblico, Siena/Scala); 74–75 Morone: *The Expulsion of the Bonacolsi in 1328 in Piazza Sordillo, Mantua*, 1494 (Palazzo Ducale, Mantua/BAL); 78 Lorenzetti: *Allegory of Good Government*, detail, 1338–40, fresco (Palazzo Pubblico, Siena/Scala); 82–83 Unknown artist (possibly by Piero della Francesca): *View of an Ideal City*, ca.1470 (Galleria Nazionale delle Marche, Urbino/BAL); 84 Giorgione (1477/8–1510): *Gattamelata (A Knight and his Page – Erasmo da Narni)*, detail (Uffizi, Florence/DO/AA); 88 The papal coat of arms on steps' pier, Todi cathedral, Umbria (BAL); 91 Mola: Helmet of Cosimo II (1590–1621),1608, steel, copper and gilded silver (Museo Nazionale del Bargello, Florence/BAL); 92 Carpaccio: *Departure of the English Ambassadors*, detail, from the St Ursula Cycle,1498 (Accademia, Venice/BAL); 94 Uccello: *Sir John Hawkwood*, 1436, fresco (Florence cathedral/BAL); 98–99 Uccello: *Battle of San Romano*, detail, c.1438–40, once owned by Lorenzo de Medici (National Gallery, London); 102 Poli (1680-1739): *Battle of Pavia in 1525*, detail (Civiche Racc d'Arte, Pavia/AA); 105 Ghiberti (1378–1455): David and Goliath, panel from the Gates of Paradise (East Door), Baptistery, Florence, bronze with gilding (AA); 106 Fouquet: *Charles VII*, ca.1447 (Louvre, Paris/BAL); 110 Large Deruta majolica dish with profile of Caesar, detail, early 16c. (Museo delle Ceramiche Deruta/Scala); 114 Sangiovanni (1592–1636): Lorenzo de Medici (1449–1492) welcoming the Arts and Sciences to the Florentine Court, detail (Palazzo Pitti, Florence/AA); 117 Cossa: Borso d'Este, prince of Ferrara, rendering justice: March from the Room of the Months, 1467–70 fresco (Palazzo Schifanoia, Ferrara/BAL); 118 Raphael (1483–1520): *Pope Julius II*, detail (National Gallery, London); 122 Mantegna: *Pallas Chases the Vices from the Garden of Virtue*, detail, ca.1499–1502 (Louvre, Paris/BAL); 127 Ripanda (active 1490–1530): *Hannibal in Italy during the Second Punic War*, detail, ca.1508–13 (Museo Capitolino, Rome/DO/AA); 128 Botticelli: *Minerva and the Centaur*, detail, ca.1480 (Uffizi, Florence/AA); 131 Leonardo da Vinci(1452–1519): Roaring lion, drawing (Musée Bonnat, Bayonne/BAL); 133 Strigel (1460–1528):

Maximilian I, Archduke of Austria (Holy Roman Emperor) and family, detail (Museo de Santa Cruz, Toledo/AA); 134 Marcus Aurelius receiving homage from defeated Barbarians, Roman stone relief, 176–180BCE (Museo Capitolino, Rome/AA); 140 Ghirlandaio (1449–1494): Donors Violante Bentivoglio and Elisabetta Aldobrandini, detail from altarpiece of St Vincent Ferrer (Museo Civico, Rimini/DO/AA); 148 Triumphal Arch of King Alfonso I of Aragon, Castelnuovo, Naples, 1453–58 and 1465–71 (Scala); 152 Berruguete (ca.1450–1504): Federico da Montefeltro, Duke of Urbino and his son Guidobaldo, detail (Palazzo Ducale, Urbino/BAL Art Library); 155 Chart of the constellations of the northern hemisphere from *Phaenomena*, by Aratus of Soli, Naples, 1469. (M.389, f.3v) Possibly illuminated by Cinico, for Antonello Petrucci (The Pierpont Morgan Library, New York/Art Resource, New York/Scala); 156 Bigarny (c.1470–1543): Court of Catholic Kings (Ferdinand of Aragon and Isabella) at surrender of Granada to Castile in 1491–92, wood relief (Royal Chapel, Granada/DO/AA); 161 Bassano (1549–1592): *Victory of Venetians over Ferrarans at Battle of Polesella in1509*, detail (Palazzo Ducale, Venice/BAL); 162 Mantegna: Ludovico III Gonzaga, Duke of Mantua (talking to his secretary Marsilio Andreasi) his Family and Court, detail, completed 1474, fresco (Camera degli Sposi, Palazzo Ducale, Mantua/Scala); 165 Bembo (ca.1420–82): *People of the Court of the Sforza Family*, detail, 1465–74 (Accademia Carrara, Bergamo/BAL); 166 Vasari (1511–74): *Homage of the people to Lorenzo de Medici*, detail (Palazzo Vecchio, Florence/Scala); 170 Bembo (ca.1420–82): Francesco Sforza, Duke of Milan (Pinacoteca di Brera, Milan/BAL); 173 Tuscan School: Savonarola burnt at the stake in Piazza della Signoria, Florence, detail, 1498 (Museo di San Marco, Florence/BAL); 174 Louis XII, King of France (1462–1515) before Allegory of Good Fortune from French Ms, detail (Bibliothèque des Arts Decoratifs, Paris/DO/AA);179 Monaco: Gates of Castelnuovo showing Scenes from Ferdinand I's Struggle, Naples, 15c. bronze (Scala); 180 Gozzoli: Lorenzo the Magnificent as one of the Three Kings, from Journey of the Magi, detail, ca.1459–1462 (Palazzo Medici-Riccardi, Florence/Scala).